In Praise of Athletic Beauty

IN PRAISE OF
ATHLETIC BEAUTY

Hans Ulrich Gumbrecht

THE BELKNAP PRESS OF
HARVARD UNIVERSITY PRESS
Cambridge, Massachusetts
London, England

2006

Copyright © 2006 by the President
and Fellows of Harvard College

This work was published in a German-language edition under the
title *Lob des Sports* © Suhrkamp Verlag Frankfurt am Main 2005

PRINTED IN THE UNITED STATES OF AMERICA

Library of Congress Cataloging-in-Publication Data
Gumbrecht, Hans Ulrich.
[Lob des sports. English]
In praise of athletic beauty / Hans Ulrich Gumbrecht.
p. cm.
ISBN 0-674-02172-X
1. Sports—Philosophy. 2. Aesthetics. 3. Sports spectators. I. Title.
GV706.G86 2006
796.01—dc22   2005035016

for Christopher and our future in his hand,

for Marco who always takes us to the limit,

*remembering Hanni whose never vanishing plays
opened the world for us,*

*and for the Stanford Cardinal football teams
from the 1989 season until 2048,
in (for once) speechless gratitude*

Contents

EVERYFAN

SOMETIMES, MEMORIES come back to him from the first National Hockey League game he ever watched, back in 1988, when he still thought of himself as a young man. It was at the Forum in Montreal, an apparently unremarkable building somewhere between the center and the periphery of that city, a building that true fans of this sport used to call "the sanctuary of hockey." A strong nicotine smell from pre-ecological times had never left the Forum's mazelike interior, with its escalators, generic concession stands, winding staircases, and strangely wide spaces that felt empty even when they were filled during intermission. All around him an infinity of photos were displayed, most in colors as brownish as the walls where they hung, some in a faded black and white

—photos celebrating long-forgotten teams and individual heroes of the Canadiens. The players were all wearing jerseys, soaked with hockey glory, that people in Montreal call *la flanelle tricolore*—white or red, with a red or blue ring around the chest and a large C in the middle. The older the photos, the more the jerseys looked as though they were made of wool, and he became obsessed with imagining what it must have felt like to sweat or to be cold and wet in a woolen uniform.

Some of the players in pictures from the early twentieth century seemed to be posing with the pride of hunters, he thought, hunters whose trophies had become invisible and whose rifles had turned into hockey sticks. And of course he saw countless photos of fans and players celebrating the Canadiens' multiple Stanley Cup triumphs in the streets around the Forum, parading in open cars, sometimes sitting next to women who tried to look Hollywood-gorgeous, sometimes surrounded by men who reminded him of Al Capone. There were also pictures of street fights, but he didn't know yet that they documented a night of wild protest against a referee's decision, a night of riot that was part of the Canadiens' mythology.

This night, the Canadiens were playing their archrivals, the Boston Bruins. He remembers the final score: a 3:3 tie, after a fierce and bloody fight between the two teams' enforcers. Years later, in the sports section of the *New York Times,* he would notice the Croatian name of one of them in a headline, and go on to read that a few months after being relegated to the minor leagues, this player committed suicide in a North Dakota motel.

The one ticket he had been able to buy outside the stadium—illegally of course, because the Canadiens' games were always sold out during those years—was standing room only, which even then was the extreme exception in a hockey stadium, and for good reason. Because from where he finally stood, after climbing several staircases in the dark, it was almost impossible to follow the lightning-fast travels of the puck across the ice. So he concentrated on the Montreal goalkeeper, who, somebody had told him, was very young (one could not have guessed it, under the helmet and grotesquely padded uniform), hugely talented, and clearly the darling of the raucous crowd.

What immediately fascinated him was the goalie's tic: he would stick his head out of his shoulder pads, as turtles do when they wake from sleep. But unlike any turtle he had ever seen, the young goalie would also rhythmically throw up his chin and his entire head, as if trying to get some disjointed bone back to its natural place. Although this movement made him look like a nervous wreck, an easy victim of the Bruins' forwards, his reactions were nothing short of stunning—beyond anybody's belief. With an almost contemptuous calm that left his head movements suspended for several seconds, he caught pucks in his glove that had been fired with full power from seven or eight yards away. It was as if he had been waiting for them since the first faceoff. No fast break—and fast breaks on ice are fast indeed—seemed ever to impress him, whereas his stare made the forwards insecure. If necessary, he would make the puck disappear by burying it under his huge padded body.

The goalkeeper's name was Patrick Roy, and this young hero of the Montreal Forum would move on to become, during the nineties, one of the all-time greatest (and most controversial) players of his sport. Meanwhile, during the long Montreal winter, wherever kids were playing hockey on frozen ponds or crowded indoor rinks, at least one boy, standing upright near the net, would try to do that turtlelike tic.

*   *   *

MOVEMENTS THAT, at first, looked unfamiliar or even grotesque to him ended up becoming so appealing that they glued him to the screen for hours. Nothing was more counter to the canon of Western beauty than the hundreds of extra pounds stored under the skin and very proudly displayed by Japanese sumo wrestlers. Yet during the minutes preceding their bouts, the ritualistic choreography performed by these athletes captivated him enough to make him forget how embarrassed he was by their monstrosity. When the wrestlers started pushing and pressing each other, when their sudden bursts of violence made them lose balance, when their colossal bodies stumbled and fell outside the ring, then it dawned on him why centuries ago sumo tournaments were organized in Shinto shrines to attract the attention of the gods. And he knew that whenever he got a chance to see enough sumo, one bout after the next, and only seconds of fighting each time, cushioned between long minutes of tense waiting, he became addicted to watching it.

Never would he forget the might of the giant Akebono, the master from Hawaii, the lord of Japan, and the idol of the most stylish Japanese ladies, whom no other wrestler of his time could move nor resist. He still recalls an afternoon at Kansai Airport, while he was waiting for Akebono to appear on the screen: suddenly, as if awaking him from the deepest sleep, a Japanese flight attendant told him, with eye-winking solidarity, that it was now or never if he still wanted to go to Sydney. He would never see Akebono wrestle again. For by the time he came back to Japan, the Hawaiian *yokozuna,* the grand master of grand masters, had retired and started a quite successful new career in the advertising business.

Yes, of course he knows that sumo is an acquired taste among Westerners, so much so that some people confuse it with bad taste. To a certain extent the same is true for hockey, especially for those fights that everybody today pays lip-service to criticizing, and that no traditional hockey fan ever wants to miss (without exactly knowing wherein the fascination lies). But could anybody, East or West, resist the smooth grace of Jesse Owens's running, as it was preserved in Leni Riefenstahl's famous film of the 1936 Olympics? Owens's concentration during the seconds before each start looked so intense that it tempted him to ask whether the greatest of all human accomplishments would not be to find a way back to the one-dimensional directedness of a hunting lion, just as some modern artists have found their way back to the strength of archaic, elementary gestures. But when Jesse Owens ran and won so effortlessly, rather than beaming with pride, his face looked almost astonished, perhaps even a bit apologetic, at the superior force that seemed to carry him past his rivals. Endlessly charming Owens was for sure, with an appeal that disregarded gender difference.

He had seen this footage hundreds of times, and though there was nothing left for him to discover, he wished he had been physically present at the Berlin Olympics. He had yet to see those pictures without noticing, to his never-vanishing confusion and embarrassment, that tears came to his eyes, tears that had nothing to do with a possible sadness about the historical Jesse's not-always-happy life. Perhaps those tears defined him as an old-fashioned type of fan, now becoming as historical as Riefenstahl's film.

*   *   *

BUT IT NEED not always be stars like Jesse Owens, Akebono, or Patrick Roy. It need not always be the objectively greatest of all times and best of the world for sports to transfigure its heroes in the eyes of passionate spectators. All that it takes to become addicted to sports is a distance between the athlete and the beholder—a distance large enough for the beholder to believe that his heroes inhabit a different world. For it is under this condition that athletes turn into objects of admiration and desire.

Several times during his childhood his father had taken him to soccer games that were played away from his hometown (which, shamefully, did not have any team in the two highest national leagues), and some of the towns where they went were as unglorious as their names: Fürth, or Schweinfurt. But the Spielvereinigung Fürth

(Henry Kissinger's favorite team) had a soccer aura earned during three national championships from the early twentieth century. Other fascinations included the strange abbreviation of the club's name (SpVgg), the Irish-looking clover that was their emblem, the vague and inexplicable taboo that seemed to surround the name of the city (today he believes it came from its reputation of being both "very Jewish" and "very proletarian"), and, above all, his father's prediction that at least one of their players, his name was Gottinger, might have a great future, perhaps even a spot on the German national team.

Schweinfurt, by contrast, had neither past nor future as a team. Two famous midfielders, whose names made them sound like twins, Anderl Kupfer and Albin Kitzinger, had played for the team and for Germany in the late thirties, through World War II, and into the early fifties, but their individual accomplishments just made the Schweinfurt team of his youth look all the more mediocre. Yet Schweinfurt played first league anyway, and thus they regularly hosted some truly important teams. Around 1960, Eintracht Frankfurt once played the final of the European Championship and got crushed 3:7 by the athletic might and aesthetic glory of the then-already-aging heroes of Real Madrid—Puskas, Di Stefano, Kopa, and Gento, who were the most visible players on one of the best soccer teams ever. Humble indeed by comparison to the "Royal" club from Madrid, Frankfurt had a goalkeeper whose rather laconic-sounding name was Egon Loy. Loy was tall and not very elastic in his movements; and even when he did not face the setting sun, he wore a cap with a visorlike shield that looked as though it was made from wool, together with (rain or shine) a gray woolen sweater and knee protectors the size of orthopedic casts.

Nobody, to his knowledge, has ever sung the praises of Egon Loy's heroic saves (nor of Gottinger's passes, for that matter). In all likelihood, Egon Loy must have been a below-average player on that altogether very respectable Frankfurt team. But to the boy, he was a hero. Never will he forget the moment when, returning from a match at Schweinfurt, father and son stopped for dinner at the local tavern in a village named Werneck, and while he was eating his bratwurst and still dreaming of the game, the victorious Frankfurt players came into the inn, and tall Egon Loy walked by his table, clumsily and so close that, for a moment, the boy could have shaken his hand. Most likely Loy came into the inn with the elegant midfielder captain, Alfred Pfaff, who looked like an intellectual turned businessman, and with Pfaff's sidekick, Richard Kress, a right-wing forward whose rather plump body did not give away how fast he could run the first ten yards of a sprint for the ball. But the boy didn't see Kress or Pfaff. He only had eyes for Egon Loy, the goalkeeper whose successor and reincarnation he wanted to become.

*   *   *

THIS ALL happened several years after the German national soccer team won its first world championship, on July 4, 1954, at Bern. That event would become historically symbolic (one only has to see Rainer Werner Fassbinder's classic film *The Marriage of Maria Braun* to know this) as marking the end of the postwar period in Germany, just as the 1964 Tokyo Olympics would

do for Japan. But for the boy it was the first individual sports event he would remember, and that
was better than symbolic. As all the grown-ups
did during that rainy Sunday afternoon without
explaining why, he listened to a radio announcer
who sounded as though he had drunk too much
wine (rather wine than beer, the voice seemed to
suggest). While the boy was sitting in front of the
huge Siemens radio with its green "magic eye,"
he learned that Toni Turek was the German goalkeeper's name, that captain Fritz Walter had a
brother named Ottmar, that Helmut Rahn, a
right-wing forward, scored twice and won the
game for Germany, and that when the match was
over something fundamental had changed in the
world around him. The grown-ups jumped up and
sang a solemn song full of words he had never
heard before—it must have been the national an-
them, perhaps even that first stanza prohibited by
the Allies because of the territorial imperialism it
claimed for Germany. The mood of his parents
and their friends seemed to swing from permanently subdued to euphoric within a matter of
minutes.

A few years after almost shaking hands with

Egon Loy and probably a good decade after Germany's first soccer World Cup (now canonized as the Miracle of Bern), he watched from fifteen meters' distance as the great Uwe Seeler, Hamburg's center forward on the German national team, scored a legendary goal against a painfully helpless Loy. Seeler kicked the ball while his airborne body was horizontal, tearing his Achilles tendon with a deep, popping sound that the (no longer so little) boy had never heard before. All this happened in a Germany that had long ago left behind the shadows of the lost war, too successfully perhaps, although the Frankfurt stadium still displayed an uncomfortable architectural monumentalism that he would soon learn to associate with the clouded history of his country.

During those early years of the sixties he started listening to Armed Forces Network on his brand new transistor radio (after midnight and under the blanket, to escape his parents' detection) whenever Cassius Clay—not yet transmogrified into Muhammad Ali—defended his Heavyweight World Championship title. Clay served the announcers' need for punchlines, again and again, with unexpected rhymes, like the one the boy was so proud to understand "live" from Miami (and will never forget), right after one of Clay's KO victories over Sonny Liston: "He wanted to go to heaven, so I took him in seven." Something new entered his sports world during those private nights, something that he liked to associate (and still wants to associate) with those black GIs he saw downtown on Sunday afternoons and who came to his elementary school at recess to see their daughters and sons, because their German mothers tried to hide them from the fathers.

*   *   *

FOR THE BOY, watching sports was definitely not what intellectuals would come to call a Proustian kind of pleasure; it was not about remembering things past. Memories were secondary at best, and retrospective distance never made better what he had seen as lived experience. Sports were about being there when and where things happened and forms emerged through bodies, in real presence and in real time. Certainly, some sports memories were deeply carved into his mind and even inscribed into his body because they came with the impulse to reenact certain movements that he had never been able to enact in the first place. But while his memories remained in the background most of the time, occasionally they came up with sudden impact, convincing him, through joyful nostalgia, that nothing had ever been more intense or stressful than those moments of real presence at an athletic event. Such memories resounded with every new experience, making each event a bit more complex, more polyphone and polyrhythmic—and somehow stronger as he got older.

Present events also recharge his memories. Each hockey goalie that he watches and admires serves to burnish the icon of Patrick Roy in his mind, while Roy's shining aura gives some of his successors the chance to become a part of his ever-growing private pantheon. Memories of Jesse Owens's divine lightness make more graceful almost every young male body he sees moving through space—although at other times those memories remind him, painfully almost, of how unusual Jesse Owens truly was. Complexifying the present and recharging the past with a glorifying and sometimes sobering aura—these are the two aspects of a transfiguration that only sports can produce.

And yet he does not know (and perhaps he doesn't even need to know) why watching sports irresistibly captures the attention and imagination of so many people like himself. It is a fascination in the true sense of the word—a phenomenon that manages to paralyze the eyes, something that endlessly attracts, without implying any explanation for its attraction. Through this ability to fascinate, sports exerts a transfiguring power, drawing his gaze to things he would not normally appreciate, like grotesquely overweight wrestlers, woolen caps with shields, or half-naked bodies that hold no sexual interest.

Would this attraction become more intense if he knew its reasons? Perhaps, though in general pleasures do not need such legitimations, which can so easily degenerate into excessively good-intentioned and therefore empty words. Sports do not need this kind of wordy blessing. Still, he would not want to exclude the possibility that trying to understand his fascination may intensify his pleasure, and help him learn how to praise the achievements of his heroes, then and now.

one

DEFINITIONS

Your HERO IS A quarterback challenged by the opposing team's defense. In the last fraction of a second before being sacked, with a lineman of the other team literally in his face, he releases the ball into the open air. The world in front of you turns into slow motion, and although the ball may fly toward your section of the stadium, you cannot anticipate where exactly it will go and who may possibly be there to catch it. And so you fear, with the nervous passion of a gambler who has put all his money on one number, that a player of the other team will intercept the pass.

But while the spinning ball describes an unlikely curve before your eyes and gradually starts its descent, a player of your team, someone you had not noticed before, suddenly appears near the place where the ball will eventually come down. These two movements, the ball in the air and the running player on the ground emerging from your peripheral vision, converge in a form that reveals itself just as it begins to vanish. The receiver makes the catch, barely, but he makes it, and as he protects the ball with his elbows, he evades the coverage of the opposing team and starts sprinting in a direction that nobody (including yourself of course) would ever have predicted. For a split second, you believe that the fire in his eyes strikes your own eyes.

Between these movements, between the player's glance and your perception, the world returns to its usual pace, and you breathe very deeply, your chest almost bursting, so relieved you are, and so proud, and so hopeful after the beautiful play that has now disappeared, never to repeat itself again in real time. The stadium roars, there is no other word, with fifty thousand voices and your own, in an organswell of joy. As you leap to your feet in excitement, you feel swept away in a wave of communal happiness. Later, walking from the stadium back to your car, through the crisp air of the fall evening, exhausted as at no other time during the week, you remember that beautiful play, and once again, without any tension and anxiety over the outcome of the game, it causes your chest to rise and your heart to beat faster. In your recollection, you can recreate its form, and as you hold onto it in memory, you feel an impulse run through your own muscles, as if to embody what your hero achieved.

Now think of your other heroes: of Michael Jordan or Magic Johnson, of Pelé, Diego Maradona, Mia Hamm, or Zinedine Zidane, think of Ted Williams, Joe DiMaggio, or Roberto Clemente. If you are ready to admit that you are the average sports fan of our times, just one among the millions who watch your favorite teams, week after week, for many hours throughout the years, then you are familiar with experiences like this, and you must know the intense feelings that such an image can trigger. And at some point you have probably wondered why.

Praise

WHY SHOULD sportslovers learn how to praise athletes and their achievements? The question points in two different directions. Is there a need to praise athletes, or is it not enough that we enjoy watching what they can do? I will come back to this problem later. Now, supposing we could find a strong reason to praise athletes, why does it seem so difficult to use the right words and, above all, to hit the right tone?

Certainly, some good and often enthusiastic writing can be found in the sports sections of newspapers every day. The real problem starts when we look for praise of athletic beauty in the world of "high culture." Here, the United States seems to be an oasis in what is otherwise a wasteland. Renowned American fiction writers like Norman Mailer, Joyce Carol Oates, John Updike, and Tom Wolfe have dedicated famous essays to athletic stars, events, and environments. Others, such as Red Smith and George Plimpton, began their careers covering boxing matches and hockey games and then went on to achieve literary recognition (including, in Smith's case, being the first sportswriter to win a Pulitzer Prize). Perhaps sports commentary has become such an American specialty because of the unparalleled importance of sports in the U.S. educational system, particularly at the college level.

The picture is much less encouraging when we look abroad. And if we concentrate on academic publications, it is a wilderness in both hemispheres. In global academia, sports as a social or a cultural phenomenon is at best a marginal topic. Granted, over the past few decades it has become somewhat fashionable for the typical Western intellectual to add "sports fan(atic)" to his resume and public image; still, the typical attitude is difficult to distinguish from a narcissistic type of condescension. European intellectuals in particular hardly ever root for the teams that occupy the dreams of those they refer to as "the masses." In pulling for the forlorn and misbegotten, they turn their role as sports fan into yet another strategy for producing cultural capital in the form of social commitment—and for feeling good about themselves.

Intellectuals, East and West, have lost not just a tone of writing but an affective disposition, and both are hard to recover. Lost indeed, because it is no exaggeration (if a slight simplification) to state that European poetry began with the praise of athletes in Pindar's odes. Of course, as soon as we try to understand these exuberant poems, we realize that the athletes whom they praise never really come into focus, at least not in the way that we moderns expect. Their names and the events they won at Olympia or Delphi are barely mentioned in the titles we find in scholarly editions. The substance of Pindar's texts consists of complicated, sometimes impenetrable constructions based on mythology and theology, genealogies of athletes' families, and the history of city states they represented—so much so that some scholars have come to view these poems as the most authentic documents we have for understanding ancient Greek cosmology. What the athletes actually achieved in the stadion or gymnasion will appear, if at all, only in passing and in very general verse. Take, for instance, these lines from the Olympian *Ode on Theron of Acragas, Victor in the Chariot-Race:*

> To rule his glorious sports, where vie
> Rapid cars and feats of might.
> Set is my soul, the glories to recite.

Instead of detailed, colorful descriptions of those rapid cars and feats of might, we read primarily of the poet's will to praise.

Even more common—and without *any* visual

suggestiveness—are lists that merely register, me-
ticulously, the multiple triumphs of Pindar's athletic heroes. Diagoras of Rhodes, for example, had
not only prevailed in the boxing contest at Olympia but

> Four times o'er in famous Corinth friendly
>   fortune blessed him still,
> Once and yet again in Nemea, and on
>   Athens' rocky hill . . .
> Him the bronze of Argos, him the works on
>   Theban anvil wrought,
> Him Arcadia's prizes, and Boethia's ritual
>   games have known,
> And Pellene. Home he brought
> From Aegina triumphs six, nor other record
>   Megara's stone
> Bears of him.

Religious enthusiasm and cultural self-celebra-
tion are the dominant themes in Pindar's praise of
fifth-century BC athletes. Such gestures, so remote
from the emotions with which we experience athletic events today, make his hymns hard to understand. But there is no doubt that the poet wanted
to render the most monumental picture his lan-

guage could produce of those superb charioteers and runners, of those unbeaten boxers and wrestlers. This determination to see and to value athletic beauty as an embodiment of a culture's highest values is what I want to call *praise*. And this capacity to praise is what we have lost—to the point where the very idea can seem embarrassing to us.

Rather than praising athletic beauty, many intellectual discourses on sports today belittle and sometimes flatly denounce what famous athletes are all about. The reference to sports as the "most beautiful marginality of life," which has long been popular in Germany *(die schönste Nebensache der Welt),* may well be the most positive and sympathetic characterization we will find among representatives of high culture. "Marginality" here does not refer exclusively to sports' lack of practical functions in our everyday lives. Literature, classical music, and the visual arts share this lack with sports, though nobody would dare to call Beethoven's symphonies, Keats's odes, or Giotto's frescoes marginal. Rather, the reference to the marginality of sports functions as a good-humored warning against taking its pleasures too seriously. It may be "cool" for an intellectual to present himself as a fan of the once-cursed Boston Red Sox or the once-mythic Notre Dame football team, but to confess that watching sports is a central component of his life makes him look rather pathetic in the eyes of his colleagues.

But it gets much worse when academics actually open their laptops to write about sports. When scholars, even scholars who love sports, apply the tools of their training to athletic events, they often wind up feeling obliged to interpret sports as a symptom of highly undesirable tendencies. Some academic critiques have gone so far as to denounce sports as a biopolitical conspiracy that emerges from the delegation of state power to self-reflexive micropowers. Through practicing and watching sports, according to this view, we regulate and re-strain our bodies against our individual self-inter-est. And hardly ever is the unprecedented popu-larity of professional sports evoked by academics without immediately interpreting it as a sign of decadence or at least alienation from a supposed but never clearly defined athletic "authenticity." Even those historians and social scientists who man-age to contain this aggressive tone rarely fail to iden-tify sports as fulfilling nothing but a subordinate function within a larger or more powerful system.

For example, the great cultural historian Norbert Elias explained the early modern rise of sports as a stage in Western civilization which served to control and subjugate human bodies—a goal to which Western culture has shown permanent dedication, as we know from the work of Michel Foucault and others. In the analysis of the French sociologist Pierre Bourdieu, sports serve the cause of social differentiation and distinction; we gratefully learn from him what we have known all along, that taking up tennis or golf is useful as a tool to accelerate upward social mobility. Although, in the sober terms of statistics, the economic importance of sports is almost negligible (an advisor to a Major League Baseball franchise once told me that the annual income of the most famous professional sports organizations is smaller than that of an average department store), we have all heard—countless times, and believed—that there is nothing but financial interest behind the production of athletic events.

And how often have the 1936 Olympics in Nazi Germany been invoked in order to make a slamdunk case for sports as a tool of political manipulation—without adding the more interesting fact that it was Adolf Hitler who felt defeated by the rise of African-American athletes to international excellence and visibility in his capital? Ironically, the inverse of this view—turning sports into a medium for identification with the oppressed, as some intellectuals and scholars are prone to do—does not constitute a huge improvement in our appreciation for and praise of athletic beauty, for it is yet another case of writing about sports in the name of a nonathletic cause.

At their very mildest, social scientists and humanists, in some otherwise interesting books, try to enlighten us with their opinion that sports are something different from what they appear to be. Since the 1930s, the French anthropologist Roger Caillois has received critical acclaim for his view that athletics belongs to the dimension of "the sacred"—a thesis which boils down to the insight that athletics is a specific kind of play, and since play, like sacred ceremonies, takes place at a distance from everyday life, athletics must therefore be a dimension of the sacred. In the promised land of academic media research—Germany—it has become an uphill battle, over recent decades, to persuade any self-respecting member of the intelligentsia that sports events possess a solid primary reality beyond (or below) their presentation

as media broadcasts. To blur the difference between Nintendo and the Bundesliga, Germany's
professional soccer league, is proof that one is cut-
ting-edge. And if an academic author generously
concedes a whiff of reality, and perhaps even a
grain of intelligence, to sports, he will normally do
so with those pompous gestures of condescension
to which I have already alluded. Clearly, this is not
the challenge or the intellectual style that I am
looking for.

Why, then, do nagging complaints and arrogant
condescension prevail in sports writing by intellectuals? Why is praising sports so difficult for them?
Does it indicate an inability of academic writers to
stay focused on the movements that some of us
watch with such passion on TV or in the stadium?
The problem cannot lie in the fact that all potential objects of description are moving objects (or,
to use the philosophical term, "time objects in the
proper sense"). Music criticism and musicology
face the same difficulty with respect to events in
time and cope with it quite well, up to the highest
levels of praise. On this basis, Theodor Adorno,
one of the great philosophers of the twentieth century who tried to think about music, was able to

assign a political function to the praising of music—and for once quite convincingly so.

Several other explanations for the difficulty of praising athletics come to mind. We should take into account, for complex historical reasons, that athletics within modern Western culture is no longer a canonized phenomenon, as it used to be at least in ancient Greece. This loss of status makes it inappropriate for the custodians of high culture to praise sports; to put it in the simplist terms, it's just not their job. A more general (and convincing) reason for intellectuals' inability to praise sports is that we feel obliged to be *critical*—only and always critical. This legacy from the Enlightenment, when our predecessors saw their exclusive mission as a relentless attack on feudal society, has seriously reduced the range of permissible discourses and tasks that we are prepared to embrace. Certainly it is difficult, perhaps even impossible, to see sports as a *tool* of criticism rather than its target.

Above all, however, I think the problem that we experience in keeping our writing focused on athletic events has to do with the tradition of Western metaphysics, and the related obsession of modern Western culture to look "beyond" what it considers to be the merely material (or merely corporeal) aspects of our existence. The metaphysical world-view not only forces us to make neat distinctions between what we see as material and what we understand as spiritual in our worlds. Being metaphysical also means consistently emphasizing, privileging, and opting for the spiritual side of this divide as the more important reality. Forms produced by body movements and the presence of these bodies, an authoritative voice seems to interject, simply cannot be important enough to care about, much less write about. We desperately want athletes' bodies to be "but" the signifiers of something spiritual, or at least psychological or mental, or at the *very* least sociopolitical—a class conspiracy or that sort of thing.

Now, it would be too easy to think that writing about sports as sports is an efficient way to go against the grain of this intellectual and discursive habit. For what could it possibly mean to write about "sports as sports"? Is it not true that every interesting description will depend on the possibility of the recurring tropes of abstraction, metonymy, or metaphor? Not necessarily so, in my view, and what I am therefore obligating myself to do in this book is quite different and simple: I will try to keep my eyes and my mind focused on athletes' bodies, instead of abandoning the topic of sports by "reading" these phenomena as a "function" or an "expression" of something else. In pursuit of this intention, there is a lot to be learned from unheralded everyday sportswriting.

If I can ever manage to resist the powerful voices (or should I say the powerful drives?) of the cultural canon, the critical stance, and metaphysics, I still must make an elementary but difficult choice of subject. Should I concentrate on what it is to practice sports and be an athlete, or what it is to watch sports and be a fan? Because I simply lack competence in active sports, and yet have felt a lifelong passion for watching them, I have quite sensibly chosen the latter option. So the book you are reading is, unilaterally, a book about the pleasures of sports spectatorship, though at a later point I will describe briefly the difference I see between the ways that an experienced athlete and a mere fan watch sports events.

At the outset, I also want to emphasize that when I am actually watching sports, I am not pursuing any intellectually (or even ethically) edifying ends. I simply enjoy the moments of intensity that such events provide, and for this I am profoundly thankful to so many athletes whom I will never personally meet. But I also have some hope that the feeling of communion which overcomes me as I am rooting for my favorite teams and for my most admired heroes may be something more than just the reliving of a childish fantasy. Sometimes, the distance between myself and my athletic heroes seems to become smaller than most of us tend to assume in our everyday rationality. Perhaps we should not rule out the possibility that watching sports can allow us to be suddenly, somehow, one with those beautiful and beautifully transfigured bodies. For many years now, I have known how much I enjoy this vague and powerful feeling. I accept the risk that it might turn out to be an illusion, but at least I want to find out exactly how athletic performance can produce this feeling—or this illusion—of oneness.

A question raised at the beginning of this chapter that I have not yet answered is why we should care about praising athletic beauty at all. We certainly do not share the religious, political, and economic motivations that led Pindar do so. In his great novel *The Man without Qualities,* the Austrian author Robert Musil was obsessed with the question of whether it was possible to use the noun *genius* in the description of a racehorse. Against the opinion of most Musil specialists, I have always been convinced that there was something more subtle than a well-identifiable philosophical problem behind this obsession (the well-definable traditional problem being, can and should we strictly separate the concept of intelligence from anything physical?). What I find more interesting than this problem is the impression (and, as I said, it may just be my impression—there are competent readers who feel that his question is purely ironic) that Musil found seductive the idea of calling a racehorse a genius because by doing so he acquired the license to praise the beauty of the horse's exquisite movements without having to transform these movements into something meaningful. This possibility has fascinated some of the great mystics (not only in the European tradition), who concentrate on physical objects or physical feelings without ever completely transforming them into meaning. My reading of Musil's motivations is consistent with the fact that he was a great admirer of this mystic form of spirituality.

It is also telling that the only genre of speech for

which Aristotle, in his *Rhetoric,* did not identify a specific function was the epideictic genre, the genre of praise (or, when necessary, of blame). In a move that we can today describe as antimetaphysical, he insisted that we should not praise just the virtues of those we admire but also, and above all, their achievements. In his clear warning against the tendency to let our attention go beyond the purely material world, I see a desire to concentrate on the things that surround us and to work on our relation to them—and nothing else. Aristotle went on to observe that, through praise, we attribute "beauty and importance" to the objects of our praise, and he finished the passage on epideixis by pointing to the tropes of amplification as being appropriate for this genre—meaning that more words and more variations of certain descriptions were the best way to praise what we love.

Now, athletes will certainly not learn much (or improve their performance) from our expressions of enthusiasm about what they achieve—almost as little as those dear departed whose past lives we honor in eulogies. It is therefore tempting to imagine that the desire to praise athletic beauty arises from sheer gratitude within those who watch. Although my favorite athletes will never read how much I admire their mastery, and although I do not believe, as Pindar did, in gods who have given me the capacity to take pleasure in watching them, I still feel gratitude—a gratitude that is part of my enthusiasm—for the pleasure of watching sports. Praising athletics would allow me to express this gratitude. Something important about how we see our own existence in relation to the world we inhabit seems to be in play here—something that resists my first attempt at finding more precise answers.

But the question why we should, unconditionally, praise what we love is not the only open question. How we should go about it is another. What words might be adequate and acceptable for this task? Despite Aristotle, I do not think that discursive amplification can still serve us well today. Since the early nineteenth century, Western readers have come to mistrust hymns or odes of praise. In our present-day culture, I will place my bet on an analytical perspective. Secretly, somehow, I suspect, analysis has produced a new epideictic genre. The best critical appreciations of the visual arts, literature, and music lay open how complex on many different layers individual works are and how their function and effect depends on such complexity. This will exactly be my approach to praising the different types of sports that we enjoy watching. It will oblige me to stay focused on forms of athletic beauty in all their complexity, instead of giving in to the metaphysical urge to interpret them, and it may produce some philosophical insights that go beyond sports. Whether I am able to praise athletic beauty by analyzing it—laying open its complexity for all to see—will be one of the measures of success for this intellectual experiment.

I will start by trying to explain a decision that has been the (so far tacit) point of departure for my book, that is, I will describe what precisely I mean when—different from many other people, different even from many other sports fans—I call sports *beautiful*. This new question raises the challenge of a new definition. For figuring out what beauty means in relation to sports should be, but is not always, a necessary precondition for praising sports. On the contrary, the little praise of sports, of college sports in particular, that we can find in present-day society comes wrapped in the shallow commonplace that "a beautiful mind will inhabit a beautiful body." Very few admirers of sports take that notion seriously, because with its implicit emphasis on the "beautiful" mind it is so obviously metaphysical. As a Stanford diving coach once appropriately said, referring to the sport to which he had devoted much of his adult life: "If you want to build character, try something else."

Beauty

WE ALL KNOW sports fans who enthusiastically call a skating routine, a home run, or a basketball play *beautiful*. But most people who apply this word to sports would be hesitant, on principle, to associate their "speech act" with aesthetic experience, even if they admit that calling something *other than sports* beautiful (a flower, say, or a handsome woman) is an aesthetic experience. If you ask intellectuals why they think sports events attract so many thousands of spectators, instead of invoking aesthetics, they will most likely revert to condescending truisms from pop psychology. "Losers in life love to identify with winners in the stadium," or "Rooting loudly for a team is an easy way to let off steam," or "Competitiveness is pervasive in our capitalistic consumer society." Apparently, we not only find it difficult to praise sports; we also find it difficult to admit that the fascination with sports can have respectable roots in the realm of aesthetic appeal.

Most people who deem themselves to be cultivated tend to believe that aesthetic experiences can be triggered only by a limited set of canonized objects and situations: by books that present themselves as "literary," by music performed in concert halls, by paintings hung in museums, or dramas produced on the stage. Being very conservative about the canon allows this elite group to profit from aesthetic experience as a tool of social distinction and privilege—a tool of distinction, by the way, that the self-declared cultivated middle class increasingly likes to use as a weapon of social aggression against the "merely rich" more so than against the ignorant, poor, and oppressed. In this view, sports teams that millions of common people watch, and some multimillionaires actually own, cannot possibly be dignified enough to pass for aesthetic experience. But would it not be a utopia come true, one can object, to see massive numbers of ordinary people, along with a handful of multi-millionaires, sharing aesthetic experience? In most intellectuals' responses to this question, a wide-spread lip service to social commitment and a vis-ceral desire to keep social distances intact begin to clash in tragicomic fashion. On the other side of the cultural divide, it would never cross the minds of typical sports fans that watching their favorite teams play head-to-head can be a form of aesthetic experience. They too have interiorized this cultural distinction.

An attempt to understand the implications of the everyday use of the word *beautiful* was the point of departure for Immanuel Kant's analysis of aesthetic experience in his *Critique of Judgment,* one of the great works of Western philosophy. If, by drawing on Kant's work, I insist that watching sports does indeed correspond to the most classical definitions of aesthetic experience, it is not to give a new aura to noncanonized forms of pleasure. As I have said before, sports do not need that badge of honor—they are already wide open for everybody's potential enjoyment, and this is one of the more positive (and most frequently observed) features of athletics. Furthermore, I would never deny that watching sports has a downside: it can foster stress, aggression, addiction, and poor health habits—you name it. I only hold that these attractions (or attractive nuisances, depending on your point of view) should not distract us from the central and conceptually most obvious explanation for the widespread popularity of sports—their aesthetic appeal.

For Kant, the word *beautiful* comes from a "judgment of taste" performed in a situation of "pure disinterested satisfaction." The operative word here is *disinterested,* in its uncorrupted sense of "having no vested interest." (Some people understand the word today to mean simply "not interested," but that's not what Kant had in mind.) Seeing your team play well or watching your favorite athlete break a record will never have any objective yield in your everyday life. You may well be on a high when you leave the stadium after an exciting match and you may even feel your self-esteem boosted, but by the time you reach your car or the subway you will have cooled down enough to realize that, like every time before, there is no way you can cash out this experience of seeing your team win a victory. On your way home and the day after, you may continue to indulge in exceptional happiness about what you saw, but you will not harbor any illusions about the positive consequences of these feelings for your social status or your savings account.

This disconnectedness from everyday life is what some philosophers since the late eighteenth century have described as the autonomy or insularity of aesthetic experience. I would go so far as to claim that even athletes who clearly have something objective at stake—high school athletes who hope to be recruited for college teams, for example, or Olympic competitors who hope to land endorsements, or professional players whose value in a trade depends on their performance—forget about those outside interests in the middle of a game or competition. Although money can be a strong motivation, during a tense inning Manny Ramirez does not think about his multimillion-dollar contract when he's trying to belt the ball out of Fenway Park. Nor do the great African runners finish their marathons with such incomparable tenacity and elegance because they want to leave the threat of poverty behind. On the contrary, we know that being able to bracket—set aside—such objective stakes for the duration of an athletic performance is an important component of athletes' competence and a key precondition for their success. As they say in tennis, this capacity to disconnect from outside pressures is what allows them "to make the big points."

In a second observation, Kant emphasizes that aesthetic judgment "is neither *grounded* in concepts nor *aimed* at them." Instead, our sense that something is beautiful or not depends exclusively on an inner "feeling of pleasure or displeasure." We need no justifying concepts for this aesthetic judgment because, since normally nothing in the everyday world is at stake, we do not need to translate our personal pleasure for outsiders to understand. And since it is the everyday world that produces differences and hierarchies between individuals, it also follows that—at a distance from such differences and hierarchies—we can expect other humans to share our own judgments of taste. This third point is what Kant calls "subjective universality." He does not try to predict that everyone will come to the same aesthetic judgment about a given book, concert, or football game. What he wants to emphasize is that our individual acts of aesthetic judgment always imply the expectation, perhaps even the invitation, for everybody to agree. And indeed, over time opinions often tend to coalesce around what is beautiful and what is less so; but this is already more than Kant wanted to point to.

This certainly seems to be the case with sports. With the multiplicity of athletic events available today, it is astonishing to see how much and how often sports fans actually converge in the enthusiasm and intensity with which they experience and later remember certain key events—and this occurs despite the fact of who won or lost the competition. Ask German soccer fans over fifty, for example, what have been the greatest games that the German national soccer team ever played, and only a few of them will fail to mention (as all Italian fans would mention) the dramatic semifinal of the 1970 World Cup in Mexico that Germany lost 3:4 in overtime against Italy. Likewise, true track and field connoisseurs will invariably rank the race in which runner Roger Bannister broke through the legendary four-minute mile as one of the most glorious moments of their sport—despite the fact that many others have since surpassed his record. Admirers of boxing will never forget the drama of the three bouts between Muhammad Ali and Joe Frazier, regardless of which boxer they were rooting for (if anyone at all was rooting for Smokin' Joe Frazier). At any enent, by the criterion of subjective universality, sports certainly seem to qualify as aesthetic experiences.

Once Kant has finished his analysis of the judgment of taste, he moves on to ask what is it that we react to with an inner feeling of pleasure—what is this thing we call *beauty?* "*Beauty* is the form of the *purposiveness* of an object, insofar as it is perceived in it *without representation of an end.*" There is an intended paradox in this description. On the one hand, something does not need to have a purpose in order to be beautiful. But on the other hand, whatever we find beautiful looks as if it had a purpose (it has the form of purposiveness, says Kant). A perfectly executed quadruple axel in a figure skating routine clearly has no goal in everyday life, and yet this multiplicity of individual body movements converge in producing the impression of purposiveness. This observation is the basis on which Kant then associates art with nature: "Beautiful art is an art to the extent that it seems at the same time to be nature." For nature, too, produces the impression of purposiveness without having that as a goal. This at least is how we can make sense of Kant's argument today—Kant himself may well have explained his thesis in a somewhat different way, for eighteenth-century thinkers were more inclined than we are to attribute purposes to nature.

We frequently have the impression, when watching sports, that a beautiful play or movement just came naturally to the athlete who produced it. But should we therefore call a powerful serve in a tennis match a work of art? Kant would say this is going a bit too far. For works of art, in his view, are produced with the intention of becoming lasting objects that can be recognized as works of art. Clearly, most athletes do not have this intention when they perform, even though we may have an aesthetic experience while we watch the performance. As a dear friend and eminent art historian once confirmed, Jesse Owens's running during the final leg of the 400-meter sprint relay at the 1936 Olympics, as captured and preserved on Leni Riefenstahl's film, is as beautiful as Michelangelo's best sculptures. But that is not to say that the movements of Owens's body were—and still are, for viewers of the film—an artwork. Assigning Owens's movements a place in our imaginary art museums would merely mummify his grace, robbing it of the uncanny freshness that Riefenstahl's film has preserved—and this is the reason why I propose to keep the concept of the artwork separate from athletic performance as a candidate for aesthetic experience.

One final distinction in the *Critique of Judgment* will help us define athletic beauty, and this is the much-debated contrast between the beautiful and the *sublime*. If the beautiful, writes Kant, "concerns the form of the object, which consists in limitation; the sublime, by contrast, is to be found in a formless object insofar as *limitlessness* is represented in it." He goes on to say that the satisfaction produced by the beautiful is always connected to a quality, whereas the satisfaction produced by the sublime is connected to quantity. The sublime is "that which is *absolutely great* . . . in comparison with which everything else is small." Kant associates the concept of the sublime with "nature in its chaos and in its wildest and most unruly disorder and devastation." The sublime is that which threatens to overwhelm us, and it may therefore cause "a momentary inhibition of the vital powers," whereas the beautiful "brings with it a feeling of the promotion of life."

By these criteria, are there many athletic events that we could call sublime in the sense that they threaten to overwhelm us? Most of the moments that spectators long for fall under the definition of the beautiful rather than the sublime, it seems to me. Despite its quantitative nature, the sublime has little if anything to do with records and record breaking, for records, by definition, belong to that which is comparatively great, not absolutely great. And yet all sports fans have memories of some achievements that they believe will never have their equal. It was not Babe Ruth's impressive lifetime statistics that made him, for many fans at least, the greatest baseball player of all time but rather that one moment in 1932, in a game against the Chicago Cubs, when he "announced" a decisive home run by pointing in the direction where the ball that he was about to hit would leave the stadium. As indeed it did.

Although Toni Sailer, the triple gold medal winner in the downhill skiing events of the 1956 Winter Olympics at Cortina d'Ampezzo, would not have been able to compete with his successors of today, nobody who saw his performance can forget the absolute grace of movement that inaugurated a new style and indeed a new age in his sport. And finally, at the 1980 Winter Olympics in Lake Placid, New York, the triumph of the American hockey team, made up of college students, over the professionals on the rival Soviet team qualifies, in most people's memory, as a moment never to be equaled. Those students were far from being one of the all-time greatest hockey teams, but this was precisely why their gold medal is still remembered as "beyond any comparison." We should reserve the concept of the sublime, then, for the breathtaking singularity of events and achievements of this kind. But in general, I believe that the sublime has less of an affinity with sports than does the concept of beauty—however trendy the sublime may have recently become among professional intellectuals.

Now, even if I, with help from Immanuel Kant, have convinced you that watching sports may be a case of what philosophers call aesthetic experience, you may have found the dry precision of Kant's ar-

guments a bit *too* dry for the purpose of praising
athletic beauty. (Kant would most likely agree with
you; as I write this, I cannot help imagining that
emaciated little man shaking his head in disbelief
and rigid disapproval over this very use of his philosophy.) So I would now like to try another tack,
which may move us closer to an understanding of
the specific beauty of sports among all other varieties of aesthetic experience.

I want to relay a description of the experience of
sports as seen through the eyes of a world-class athlete, Pablo Morales, a triple gold medal winner in
swimming at the Olympic games of 1984 and 1992
and a former student of Stanford and Cornell universities who went on to become a successful law-
yer. During a panel discussion in a colloquium on
"The Athlete's Body" held at Stanford in 1995,
Morales was asked why he had decided to return
to competitive sports, which led to winning his
only individual gold medal, after having retired
and after skipping the Olympics in 1988. Here is
his spontaneous reply:

> In 1988 I didn't make the Olympic team, even
> though I was present at the prior and subse-
> quent Olympics. This year was disappointing

enough to lead to my retirement. So when I viewed the games on television, I didn't feel any special pull — until a funny thing happened. When coverage began of the one hundred meter butterfly competition, the event that was my specialty, and the one I would have had a shot at winning the gold medal, I had to remove myself from the room. I simply couldn't watch the race. My attachment to the event was so complete that viewing it proved impossible.

The meaning of this experience became clearer to me when I saw the 400-meter sprint relay for women. I will never forget watching the great sprinter Evelyn Ashford run as, in the anchor leg, she came from behind to win the gold medal for the United States. The race was shown through to its conclusion, after which a replay was run but this time with the camera focused on Ashford's face before, during, and after her sprint. Her eyes first panned the oval, then focused on the baton, then on the curve ahead. Oblivious to the crowd, oblivious even to her competition, I saw her lost in focused intensity. The effect was immediate. I had to remove myself from the room once again. I went into the kitchen and started sobbing, without knowing why. I had not a single emotional outburst since failing to make the Olympic team. But when I thought about my reaction in the ensuing hours, I came to realize what I had lost; that special feeling of getting lost in focused intensity. Four years later I was back at the Olympics.

In this moving narrative, Morales does not draw a line between his experience as a spectator and his experience as an athlete. On the contrary, what he saw on the television screen helped him to grasp, for the first time, what had motivated him to practice sports at the highest level. To be *lost in focused intensity* is the stunning, complex, precise formula through which he links the fascination of watching sports with the motivation of performance.

Lost, the first word of this formula, I understand as the equivalent of Kant's insistence on disinterestedness. Just as the person who performs an aesthetic judgment feels disconnected from the opinions of the world around him, so the athlete

Evelyn Ashford appeared to be "oblivious to the crowd, oblivious even to her competition." She was alone with herself, lost to the world, disconnected from all the goals that made up her everyday life, even from the goals that—extrinsically or intrinsically—belonged to the athletic event in which she participated.

To describe what Morales identifies as Ashford's feelings, both her emotions and the perception of her own body, he used the word *intensity*—a heightening of qualities and impressions that always already exist for us. From this we can conclude that athletic experience—and aesthetic experience in general—is not qualitatively different from our experience in other less marked situations. What is different is that our physical and emotional capacities are operating close to their maximum.

Focused intensity encompasses not just the ability to exclude a multiplicity of potential distractions but also a concentrated openness for something unexpected to happen. Something whose coming is not under our control and will therefore always appear to be sudden. Something which, as soon it unexpectedly appears, will begin to disappear, irreversibly and often painfully because we want to hold onto the pleasure and possibility that it offers.

There seem to be players whose performance capitalizes on their openness to sudden moves that arise seemingly out of nowhere. Think of the great Diego Maradona's sprints through the opposing defense and how they were surrounded by long minutes in which he seemed to have disappeared from the field. Recall the incomparable striker Gerd Mueller of the 1970s, who was really in the game only when he scored one of his innumerable goals (the most valuable being Mueller's sudden appearance in the penalty zone, thanks to which a hopelessly inferior German team beat the Netherlands for the World Championship of 1974). Think of Shaquille O'Neal's huge body becoming invisible just in the seconds before he rises up to slamdunk the ball once again. The action of stealing a base in a baseball game embodies and, paradoxically, institutionalizes this interplay between invisibility and sudden threat. To play with a runner on base makes a pitcher nervous because the suddenness of the runner's potential action is beyond his control and virtually invisible. Each time that a player tries to steal a base he emerges, almost literally, out of nowhere.

This unexpected appearance of a body in space, suddenly taking on a beautiful form that just as quickly and irreversibly dissolves, can be thought of as a kind of epiphany. Such epiphanies are, I believe, the source of the joy we feel when we watch an athletic event, and they mark the height of our aesthetic response. They throw us into an oscillation between our perception of the sheer beauty of the physical form and our obligation to interpret that form according to the rules of the particular game. Anyone who has followed a game of American football from the sideline knows that one cannot help perceiving the players' clashing bodies, in all their potential violence, as a physical threat. But at the same time, one cannot avoid attaching meaning to their movements: we say the receiver held onto the ball, for a gain of thirty-five yards and a first down. And yet the meanings we attribute to bodies and movements can never fully account for the emotional impact of their physical presence.

Pablo Morales's short, compact narrative suggests that experiencing sports, being lost in focused intensity, both as an athlete and as a spectator, can lead to addiction. This is the reason why he had to come back from his retirement. But Morales does not say what content, what object exactly motivates this addiction, and Kant's attempts at describing the object of aesthetic pleasure are among the less successful parts of his analysis. As we seem to have neither philosophical nor athletic authorities to invoke in order to answer the question of what makes athletic beauty so addictive, I will have to call upon my own very subjective memories and expectations.

My moments of being lost in focused intensity while watching sports, moments when my attention grows sharper and my emotions become overwhelming, are always accompanied by a feeling of composure (interestingly, the German word for *composure* is *Gelassenheit,* "the capacity of letting be"). The euphoria of focused intensity seems to go hand in hand with a peculiar quietness. I am at peace with the impression that I cannot control and manipulate the world around me. So intensely quiet do I become and so quietly confident, at least during the seconds when my favorite football team is talking through its next play in the huddle, that

I feel I can let go and let come (or not) the things that I desire to come. I am open to the next experience, whatever it may be. Great athletes share this attitude of composure with the most concentrated spectators. But in the athletes' case, composure is a precondition of their capacity to make things happen, rather than to let things happen. Perhaps this condition is best phrased in the form of a paradox: great athletes make things happen by letting things happen to themselves.

What I am trying to describe, on the spectators' side, is by no means a learned response to the inevitable disappointments all fans endure. I am not trying to say that the bitter defeats of my favorite teams have taught me to take the hit with a stiff upper lip. Rather, I feel drawn into an openness toward the material world around me, into an openness that makes my own volition and my claims to agency appear marginal, vague, and almost random. For not only am I aware that I have no influence on the agility and endurance of the boxer I want to win; it is even out of my control how intensely I will react to his performance.

The question remains, now that we have tried to explain under which subjective conditions we call sports beautiful, whether there is anything intrinsically specific about *athletic* performance as an object of aesthetic experience. Something specific that could "objectively" account for its irresistible appeal and for its so often overwhelming impact. In other words: does the specific form of athletic performance produce a specific form of aesthetic effect?

Athletics

THIS TIME, the task seems to be quite clear and straightforward. In order to say what different sports have in common and how they can all be beautiful in so many variant ways, we must come up with a definition of athletics. But while the task looks uncomplicated at first glance, it will turn out to be unusually difficult. Nevertheless, I hope you will stay with me as we work through this last of my three definitions, because the general terms I introduce here—performance and presence, *agon* (competition) and *arete* (striving for excellence), tragedy and transfiguration—will be critical in our explorations of more specific and familiar topics in the chapters that follow.

The problem of definition starts, in English, with our use of the plural forms (sports, athletics). In the *Oxford Universal Dictionary* the definition of *sports* is "participation in games or exercises, esp. those pursued in the open air"; or "such games collectively." The same dictionary describes the meaning of the singular *sport* as a "pleasant pastime, amusement." But of course we tend to think of all sports as potentially pleasant and amusing, and the restriction to open air, if we took it seriously, would exclude some forms of amusement that are part of the world of sports, like sumo or even chess. Yet, if we consider for a moment such activities as dressage, soccer, rugby, and wrestling, we begin to have some sympathy with the *Oxford* definition writers. It is indeed very difficult to come up with more than two or three (if any) very general properties that these four sports share.

Instead of thinking about sports as a set of phenomena that are all rooted in a common denominator, we would probably be wise to imagine sports as a network of practices related through what Ludwig Wittgenstein famously called a family resemblance. In a family resemblance, item A shares some features with item B, and item B shares some features with item C. And even though A and C may have no features in common, their shared resemblance to B keeps them all in the family. Wrestling and rugby certainly have some affinities in common, and rugby and soccer developed from the same group of games. But wrestling and soccer do not visibly share a lot of features, and the convergence of dressage and soccer is even harder to see. Yet all fall under the rubric of sports. So what we are seeking is not an all-comprehensive definition of athletics but one that simply allows us to see them all as interconnected.

To make matters more complicated, I would also insist that we need a workable definition of athletics that does justice to their aesthetic appeal, from the spectator's perspective. As with opera, symphony, or ballet, spectators in the stadium experience sports as a performance—but a particular kind of performance that differs from these other aesthetic experiences. Now, as many intellectuals are quick to point out, the word *performance* has received much attention of late, in both the social sciences and the humanities, and a rich, diverse literature has grown up around this concept. Yet the definitions I found in a number of recent encyclopedias and specialized dictionaries were incoherent, to say the least. Most of them mention the same three components of performance: its "body investment," its "event character" (which is meant to set performance apart from anything that emerges through writing), and its use of "material objects." But do all types of performance really involve material objects? Of course not. And is it essential (or even adequate) to exclude writing from performance? No.

After offering such ultimately unsatisfactory conceptual proposals, some of the entries on performance jump to exemplify what they have failed to define by pointing to highly canonized examples of Modern art. John Cage's experiments with sound and music or Jackson Pollock's action painting come to stand in as (implausible, in my opinion) replacements for the definitions that those entries neglect to offer. If you like to work with dictionaries and encyclopedias, you may be familiar with my frustration: between conceptual solutions that are too general and examples that are too

specific, their definitions often leave blank the se-
mantic space we had expected them to fill.

Disappointed in these attempts to clarify what
performance might be, I became interested in the
concept of *presence* as a possible opening or approach to the problem (the problem being, you
will recall, to define athletics in such a way as to
take into account its aesthetic attraction). So what
is presence? What do we mean when we say somebody has presence? Surprisingly perhaps, presence
emphasizes space much more than time (the Latin
word *prae-esse* literally means "to be in front of").
Something present is something within reach,
something that we can touch, and of which we
have immediate sensual perceptions. Presence in
this sense does not exclude time, but it always
binds time to a particular place.

But I am rushing ahead of myself. To get a better grip on what I mean by presence, we might
contrast it with a different dimension, which I will
call *meaning*. I can see at least seven polar differences between presence and meaning. We might
start with our everyday belief, following René Des-
cartes, that "I think, therefore I am" *(Cogito ergo
sum)*. This notion, consistent with the meaning di-

mension, posits the mind as the exclusive guaran-
tor of the reality of human existence; the body (the
res extensa, the thing that occupies space, as Des-
cartes called it) does not play any role in this self-
referential worldview. In the presence dimension,
by contrast, while human self-reference does not
exclude the mind, it always attributes primary importance to what the body knows. When Pablo
Morales described the sprinter Evelyn Ashford, he
implied that at the moment of taking over the
baton, her concentration was fully focused on her
body and its perceptions, not on the "higher" analytical or verbal functions we normally characterize
as thoughts.

Second, when people conceive of themselves
primarily as mind, they necessarily see the world of
physical objects from a position of distance. And
then, as distanced observers, they engage in interpreting those objects by assigning different meanings to them. In the presence dimension, by contrast, people feel that they are part of and
contiguous with objects in the physical world. It
would not occur to a soccer player to ask himself
what the ball could possibly "mean." He will simply touch the ball, caress it, as his fans sometimes

say with tender admiration, and this gentle motion ultimately makes the ball arrive at an unexpected place on the field. The metaphor of having "the ball glued to his foot" that we like to use for soccer players like Zidane or Beckenbauer is quite telling here.

A third contrast arises from the fact that, in the meaning dimension, after people have interpreted objects, they tend to try to transform them and the world they occupy. When people carry out such intentions (projects), we call their behavior an *action*. Unintuitive as it may seem at first, the presence dimension has no place for action in this sense. People operating in the presence dimension do not aim beyond inscribing their bodies and their behaviors into certain regularities that they believe to be inherent in the world of objects. This inscribing is sometimes called a ritual, and in the case of sports we call the ritual a game. Great athletes are not great because they change the rules of the event in which they excel. Rather, they mostly try to reach—and sometimes to move—the limits of what is possible within a stable set of rules and recordkeeping. Associations like the Fédération Internationale de Football Association (FIFA) get it right when they are so very conservative about the rules of their games. The steroid scandal in American baseball is troubling in large part because it makes comparison of athletes' records over time impossible.

The fourth contrast will not be to the taste of those sports enthusiasts who pride themselves on being purists. This contrast is about the display of violence—the moment of occupying or blocking spaces with bodies, against the resistance of other bodies. The presence dimension allows for and sometimes indulges in violence, whereas the meaning dimension emphasizes power (social, political, economic, psychological power as a mere potential of violence) over real violence. But many sports cannot exist without physical violence, or at least the threat of violence. I am not speaking only of boxing and American football, whose central movements—and whose glory—consist of violent contact. The elegance of the greatest players in basketball or soccer also depends on adeptly evading or bypassing the violence of those who want to stop them. What would Mané Garrincha, the best player of all time on the right wing of the soccer game, have been without hundreds of defenders who very visibly and desperately tried to stop and even to foul him but failed, and whose violence therefore never hit its target? Muhammad Ali's famous motto, "Float like a butterfly, sting like a bee," highlights the equivalent moves of avoiding the opponent's violence in a boxing match and, in so doing, opening up opportunities to play out one's own violent potential.

Distinction number five can be described as two different types of *eventness*. In the meaning dimension, we consider an event to be an incident that marks the beginning of a new and more or less profound transformation. In the presence dimension, however, *every* beginning, even a beginning that endlessly repeats itself or was long anticipated, has the status of an event. We know that in most games of the National Hockey League the puck will drop for the first face-off at exactly 7:35 p.m. But this absence of newness does not make the initial face-off less exciting. On the contrary, in the presence dimension we appreciate the tension and excitement that lies in this predictable moment of discontinuity when the promised and expected finally become the real event. Eventness, in this dimension, may entail some innovation or transformation, but it does not rely on them.

The sixth distinction features the concept of play. Some classics of sociology define play—in contrast to action—as mutually adapted sets of behavior whose participants have but vague motivations or no motivations at all. Since motivation, in this definition, refers to the intention of transforming the world through purposive behavior, a lack of such motivations makes play less serious, when viewed from the dimension of meaning. But this contrast between playfulness and seriousness makes no sense in the presence dimension, which neutralizes the distinction because presence does not include a place for action. While we call the participants in an athletic event *players,* we know that those players would not perform well if they were not serious about the game. Indeed, if any of them did not try his or her best, this would immediately lead to the end of the game.

"It's only a game" is a saying we can apply once the event is over, but not before. Nothing is ever fictional in the presence dimension, even a sports event such as Hulk Hogan's "wrestling." Though his behavior is obviously a fiction when seen from the meaning dimension, during the actual events the Hulk, like performers in the theater, has to avoid all possible hints at the fictive character of his fights and tantrums. It is his sense of presence that makes his fans so willing to suspend their disbelief. In sports as in the dramatic arts, everything is real during the performance, nothing is mere play or pretend—for what could it mean to say, for example, that swimmers in a race are merely playing, or that they are only pretending that it matters to move fast in the water?

The last item on my list contrasts the way the sign is defined and used in the meaning dimension and the presence dimension. As most college students learn nowadays, a sign relates a material signifier (a sequence of sounds or of characters) to a meaning, and it normally brackets the physical object (the "referent") to which a signifier may refer through a meaning. This is why we say that signifiers carry or express meanings. As a sequence of sounds or of traces on the paper that point to a meaning, every word in every language is of course a signifier in this sense—even if it is not connected to an individual referent outside the language in question (which may well, and often, be the case). But the exclusion of material referents in the world does not operate in the presence dimension. Here, we need a different concept of the sign—for example, the one offered by the Aristotelian tradition. This sign concept connects matter or substance (that which occupies space) with form (that which makes it possible to perceive, at any given moment, whatever occupies space). It does not separate a purely material from a purely nonmaterial side, and we therefore do not arrive at a neat distinction between meaning and the material objects that articulate meaning. Water as it adapts itself to the form of any given recipient while it maintains its volume would be the most elementary illustration of this phenomenon.

Counter to many academic (and highly incompetent) "readings" of sports, athletic competitions do not express anything and therefore do not offer anything to read. They fascinate us with bodies "that matter" (a useful pun invented by the philosopher Judith Butler), bodies that adapt themselves to multiple forms and functions. By interpreting these bodily forms and functions and transforming them into meanings, we run the risk of reducing, if not destroying, the unique pleasure we take in athletic events.

Drawing from this list of distinctions between presence and meaning, I propose that we may call any human body movement a performance as long as we see it, predominantly at least, in the presence dimension. For I believe that we hardly ever watch sports from any other angle. This definition of performance certainly does not imply that there are no "actions" taking place on a soccer field; it only means that seeing the athlete's movements as transformations of his world—that is, asking ourselves what a player's intention may possibly be while he throws or kicks the ball—is not what we mainly do when we become sports spectators.

Of course this definition does not imply that we can now subsume all kinds of performance under the concept of athletics. Performance and athletics are not coextensive. Therefore, we have to continue our inquiry and ask what makes sports specific within the seeming infinity of possible modes of performance? In doing so I want to take up two concepts that the Western intellectual tradition offers as potential tools for this next step toward a definition of athletics. Both of them come from ancient Greece, but it is hard to tell how much their present-day use was shaped by the nineteenth-century waves of phil-Hellenic enthusiasm. The concepts in question are *agon* and *arete*.

Agon is perhaps best translated simply as competition. Among other things, we associate competition with the domestication of potentially violent fights and tensions through institutional frames of stable rules. Arete, by contrast, means striving for excellence with the consequence (rather than the goal) of taking some type of performance to its individual or collective limits. (The U. S. Army's slogan "Be all you can be" draws on the idea of arete.) Now, I am well aware that most people—specialists, enthusiasts, and outsiders alike—would identify agon rather than arete as the dominant component of athletic performance. Going against the grain, I choose arete, without of course excluding all elements of agon, and for two very different reasons. Above all, I prefer arete because I think that striving for excellence always implies competition, whereas competition does not necessarily imply striving for excellence. Arete, then, is the more specific concept. For even if we strive for excellence in absolute solitude, we cannot do so without competing against the performance of (absent) others.

Paavo Nurmi, the world-leading long-distance runner of the 1920s, was famous for breaking world records in lonesome races against the stopwatch, and this meant, at least while he was at the height of his career, that he was running against his own previous records. At Oxford in the spring of 1954, when Roger Bannister became the first athlete to break the four-minute-mile barrier, the only people on the track with him were two pacemakers; but he was really running against the existing and the potential records of his competitors thousands of miles away, in Australia and the United States. On the other hand, it is possible and indeed quite common to compete against others without testing one's limits. In every league and at every track and field meet, matches and events take place in which the winners do not face any serious challenge. These are competitions, but they do not oblige superior athletes or superior teams to test their limits.

The second reason why I opt for arete over agon has nothing to do with the problem of defining athletics per se, but rather with the goal of praising athletic beauty. If I were to praise competition rather than excellence, I would confirm a vision of sports that has given them a bad reputation among so many intellectuals. This is the image of athletes and their fans as a bunch of nail-biting, anxiety-driven neurotics, addicted to a competitiveness spawned of capitalism and warped by the stress that such competitiveness is supposed to produce. Striving for excellence and testing one's limits, however, cut right through all these negative associations, and project a much nobler—or at least a much less condescending—vision of sports.

Let me insist that I am not interested in eliminating or even setting competition to one side. Arete and agon go together in most athletic events —and certainly in all of the most popular events. All that I want to secure, against a certain discursive tradition, is an adequate consideration of arete. Where agon and arete converge is in the athletic drive to go further, to go where no body has ever gone before. Such an aggressive drive does not spare the potential loser's feelings, either emotionally or physically. Fair play in athletics can never mean giving your opponent an advantage. Rather, it is the capacity and generosity of sympathizing with the pain and the tragedy of the person you beat in a fair fight. It is the respect Achilles showed for the defeated Hector, not Jesus' injunction to turn the other cheek.

Spectators prefer to watch athletes as they test and push the absolute limits of human performance. And in most sports, this desire to see the very best athletes perform presents a problem for minor leagues and, unfortunately, for some women's sports. Women's soccer may often be more beautiful than men's soccer, and women's basketball may sometimes reach higher levels of strategic sophistication than men's basketball. Yet many spectators (and I admit to being one of them) simply cannot forget that the best men's teams would prevail over the best women's teams. Here, we reach the limit of arete as the central fascination of athletics and are forced to concede the attraction of agon.

Women's performance in some sports, like gymnastics or figure skating, does not encounter this limitation. For me, the most interesting event in this context is women's tennis as it has developed over the past two decades. Although there is no doubt that the best female tennis players do not stand a chance yet to beat the male champions in a competitive match, I find a grace, agility, and tenacity in women's tennis that allow me to imagine a reversal of powers in the future. But maybe I just want to imagine such a future because I hate to admit that gender asymmetry in sports points out the impossibility of fair play in certain situations.

So how can college football and college basketball be so very popular, you may ask, if we know that those teams would not stand a chance to win against their professional counterparts? There is certainly no other sport that I watch with more passion than college football. An easy way out would be to refer, once again, to the popularity of college sports as an American exception. But what matters above all, I believe, is knowing that the best college players in football and basketball will be tomorrow's professional stars. As this is much less consistently the case with college baseball, the numbers of spectators in that sport cannot compare to those of college basketball and football.

The issue of fair play raises the question whether the tragedy of the loser can ever be embodied in an aesthetically appealing form. The most cherished baseball memory of my friend Eiko Fujioka from Osaka is precisely about the grace of a tragic loser, and it makes me hope, once again, that a level exists—and it may well be the highest level of athletic achievement—where arete, very visibly, dominates over agon:

> I still remember when, about fifteen years ago, I became a fan of Koji Akiyama who then played for the Seibu Lions. I was watching a game of the Japan championship series on TV. Akiyama stepped up to the batter's box with two or three players on base and two outs. This was a big chance to make another score. The pitcher got two strikes. Then, with the next pitch coming in a really tense situation, Akiyama didn't swing—and it was a strike. He got struck out. He missed making another score for his team in this very important game. The stadium was filled with a big sigh of disappointment from the Lions fans. In this situation, Akiyama stayed at the batter's box a second longer than he needed to—and gave a really beautiful smile to the pitcher.

Akiyama's smile, I believe, must have come from the feeling that, for a brief moment at least, the opposing pitcher had taken the game of baseball to its highest level, making him, the man at bat who lost the competition, part of this achievement. It was like the smile of the angels that we see sculpted into the stone of medieval cathedrals—art historians believe these smiles signify the angels' happiness at being able to play a role in God's perfect creation. Akiyama's happiness over being allowed to play his role in a splendid situation of arete ended up being greater than the frustration over his own loss, perhaps even greater than his joy over a win would have been.

The rules of different sports determine, explicitly and implicitly, the ways in which an athlete may try to compete and excel, and by extension what movements a spectator can find beautiful. The longer the rules of a specific sport have remained unchanged, the more impressive the latest record-breaking performance will be. During the 2003–2004 season of the English Premier League, the soccer team of Arsenal London was unbeaten. The best way to underscore the greatness of this performance is to say that no other team had been equally successful since Preston North End in 1888–1889.

Obviously, athletic rules and regulations do not

solely exist for the purpose of making such comparisons possible. So what are they good for? In everyday life, if I want to persuade a merchant to give me a discount, I do not need a set of rules to go by—the form of my action will follow naturally from my intention. But how would a group of young men go about measuring their physical fitness against one another if they did not have the rules of rugby or basketball or Australian football to constrain and direct their play? Making both agon and arete possible, the rules of different sports confirm and consolidate the insularity that separates athletics from the everyday world. Each set of rules is meaningless except in an actual competition. Outside a track and field event, it does not make sense to throw heavy iron balls into empty space—not even in wartime. For the athlete and his spectators, the pointlessness of such rules within the everyday world is a precondition for becoming lost in focused intensity during the event.

The chance to win and the risk of losing produce narrative, epic, and drama. And while the intense desire to enjoy victory certainly motivates athletes to enter a competition and spectators to root for them, I believe that the motivation of win-

ning has been overrated, above all in comparison
with the impact that the dramatic dimension has
on the way we see and remember athletic events.
But what exactly does "drama" mean here? Bor-
rowing a concept from the language of Christian
theology, we can perhaps say that the drama of
competition is responsible for the transfiguration
of great athletes within our immediate perception
and, later, our memory. A person who has been
transfigured appears to be removed from his or her
original place. In the New Testament, when the
disciples followed Jesus "to a high mountain," they
saw before them the shining bodies of Jesus, Mo-
ses, and Elijah. Likewise, athletic competition can
transfigure bodies and their movements, making
them shine in the particular light of triumphant
victory or tragic defeat. Rather than assigning specific meanings to bodies and their movements, victory or defeat gives them something like what the
Christian tradition used to call a halo—and what
today we might call an aura.

Or to use a word that was in high esteem among
artists and critics during the early twentieth century, we may say that through the transfiguring
lens of victory or defeat we remember certain ath-

letic movements as dramatic *gestures.* More so than
a halo or aura, a gesture captures, in a specific, con-
cise movement, a critical moment in a dramatic
narrative. Gestures, with their freeze-frame effect,
make the pathos associated with these dramatic
moments more visible and more memorable. They
are like material signifiers that appear to be permeated by specific meanings, and they thus become
signifiers whose materiality exceeds the function of
just carrying a meaning. Often we remember great
athletes of the past and the present in this transfigured way. Roger Federer, the great Wimbledon
champion of the early twenty-first century from
Switzerland, is such a case. We associate elegance
and effortlessness with his flowing movements on
the court that never seem to be centered on just
one play. But the form and the rhythm of these
movements, as an object of our perception and of
our memory, tend to become independent of what
we might read into them. They are unique, and
they symbolize—by transfiguration—what we call
"vintage Federer."

Transfiguration does not surround with light
only those who win. I will never forget the profound sadness that came over me when I watched

the players of my favorite college football team, the Stanford Cardinal, leave the stadium after the worst home defeat in their more than 100-year history, in a late November game against Notre Dame. The rhythm of their steps seemed strangely solemn, their eyes were distant, searching the most removed horizon, the sweat had drawn gray shades into their hair. One of my favorite players, Michael Lovelady, looked like a king who was leaving his country for a humiliating exile. I am not embarrassed to say that this was a Shakespearean moment for me. Michael Lovelady did not resume his promising football career the following season.

There are many individual athletes and teams whose charisma depends on having failed—tragically failed—to win any great competition during long years of indisputable excellence. Raymond Poulidor, a French bicycle racer in the 1960s, never managed to win the Tour de France, but the fans loved and revered him more than his antagonist, Jacques Anquetil, who, during the same years, triumphed at the Tour a then-record five times. And in the summer of 2004, no other baseball franchise, not even the fabled New York Yankees, could compete with the popularity of the Boston

Red Sox, a team that had not won a single World Series since 1918.

The team's tragic myth was born in 1919, just one year after winning their first Series, when the Red Sox traded their best player, 25-year-old Babe Ruth, to the New York Yankees, which went on to become the most successful baseball club in history. In baseball mythology, the Babe cursed the Red Sox for not coming to terms with his volatile temperament. Year after year, the Red Sox' excellent lineups seemed unable—or perhaps unwilling—to break the Curse of the Bambino. In the fall of 2003, when they faced the Yankees in the American League postseason playoffs, their best pitcher at that point—and certainly one of the better pitchers of our time—Pedro Martinez, inexplicably lost control over both his composure and his pitching skills, which led ultimately to a Yankees victory in the World Series.

In the following summer, a few months before the Red Sox would beat the Yankees to win the American League pennant and go on to win the Series, I confess that the names of the 2004 Red Sox' greatest players—Johnny Damon, David Ortiz, Manny Ramirez, and Pedro Martinez—

sounded like verses from a Greek tragedy to me. Even the turning event, their come-back victory over the Yankees, seemed to fully exploit the potential of a tragic history transfigured. The Red Sox had lost the first three games of the seven-game play-off series, reaching what appeared to be a humiliating low point at the end of a devastating home defeat in Boston's Fenway Park. Everybody expected the next game in New York to clinch the win for the Yankees. The Red Sox and their fans entered Yankee Stadium with only the faintest hope of regaining a shred of their lost dignity with this one win. But they won four games in a row, and, never looking back, took four games from St. Louis to win the World Series championship,

Never looking back, really? Has the 2004 championship changed the Boston Red Sox forever? This is a difficult question, too early to ask perhaps, and certainly too early to answer. Conceivably, the Red Sox might become the powerhouse of the future, but I find this unlikely. It is easier to imagine that the 2004 championship was a necessary event within the narrative economy of a specific mythology, the mythology of losing with drama and dignity, and that the Yankees' defeat was a necessary condition for their own future triumphs—which, if they came too easily, would not really be triumphs at all.

During the early 1950s, the Hungarian national team dominated European soccer, not only in a long series of undefeated matches but through the powerful elegance of its playing style and with a number of unforgettable individual players. Fulfilling the highest expectations, they beat Germany in the first round of the 1954 World Cup in Switzerland, by the hyperbolic margin of 8:3. With uncanny luck, Germany then survived the elimination round and played Hungary again, only two weeks later, in the championship match, beating everybody's favorite team by a score of 3:2. This was the victory that Germans hailed as marking the end of the postwar period. Hungarian soccer never returned to its former eminence, and for many—in Hungary and outside—the epic defeat of 1954 turned into a retrospective premonition (the paradox is intended) of the atrocity of 1956, when Soviet tanks repressed a movement for national independence in the streets of Budapest.

Of course a habit of losing decisive games or big points will not, alone, guarantee the kind of cha-

risma that the Boston Red Sox or Hungary's legendary soccer team enjoyed. A German soccer
franchise, Bayer Leverkusen, has managed, several
times within a few years, to lose championships literally during the last minutes of the season. But
rather than becoming popular, Bayer Leverkusen
has become the laughingstock of an entire nation—while almost nobody, not even New York
Yankees fans, would ever have dared to enjoy a
laugh at the expense of the Boston Red Sox. And
nobody who remembers the Hungarians' defeat of
1954 ever speaks of it without respect or even re-
gret.

two

DISCONTINUITIES

MANY FANS IMAGINE that the history of athletics spans more than two and a half millennia, from the ancient Olympics, through their 1896 revival, to the mega-events of today's college, amateur, and professional sports. The only important change in this history, most people believe, is the effect of decay—the impression that a primordial authenticity has somehow been progressively attenuated or even lost. When the Baron de Coubertin launched the idea of revitalizing the Olympic games, he did so because he too believed in the continuum between ancient and modern sports—a favorite illusion of late-nineteenth-century Europeans. Though traces of this romantic view can still be discerned today, the history of sports in fact, as I will try to show, is, rather, fraught with striking discontinuities.

In the previous chapter I proposed a definition of athletics based on three components. Above all, whatever we call sports, in my view, is a form of performance, by which I mean any kind of body movement seen from a perspective of presence. Among the many phenomena that qualify as performance, the forms of athletic performance are specific because they are permeated by the values of agon (competition) and arete (striving for excellence). And finally, what I call sports will always appear to be at a distance from the interests and strategies that make up our everyday world. Each of these features of sports at various times has presented an obstacle to the historical continuity of sports.

In the first place, if the importance of performance and presence varies among different historical cultures, then it follows that the likelihood for body movements to be experienced as sports must have constantly varied over time as well. Not only (and perhaps not even primarily) in the sense that cultures with strong presence components may have had a greater affinity for sports. The inverse possibility also exists (probably our own time is one such example): that a *scarcity* of presence components in everyday life may produce an overwhelmingly strong desire to see the world from an angle of presence. For what we most desire is almost always what is the hardest to obtain.

As for agon and arete, I agree with the great nineteenth-century historian Jacob Burckhardt, who wrote, in his *History of Greek Culture,* that in certain historical moments individuals have a greater tendency to compete and to strive for excellence than in some others. We may never completely understand why the spirit of arete and agon emerges in one cultural context and vanishes in another, but that it does seems beyond doubt to me.

Finally, the ability of sports to achieve a distance from everyday life depends on socio-structural conditions that are subject to enormous variation. It is hard to imagine that peasants in medieval times, when physical exertion was a daily requirement for survival, shared our modern fixation with recreational exercise and sport. In modern societies, by contrast, sports enjoy a high degree of presence-centered insularity from the everyday world—an insularity that is vital to the focused achievements of athletes and the aesthetic enjoyment of fans. But at the same time, this autonomy stands in complex tension with meaning-centered enterprises on which major league franchises, university development offices, municipal governments, sports media, athletic equipment and clothing industries, even the medical/pharmaceutical/surgical establishment also depend. The exact equivalent to our modern experience of sports as removed from (and at the same time connected to) everyday life cannot have existed in less meaning-heavy cultures.

Many individual sports of the past seem to have emerged suddenly, in an eruption of institutional structures, and to have disappeared just as quickly. The more we learn about the contexts of boxing in ancient Greece or of *calcio* in Renaissance Italy, the less convinced we become that they are predecessors of modern boxing and soccer. Understanding this discontinuity in the historical dimension is important, because it allows us to ask how it was possible—historically possible, I mean—that sports became so expansive and so important in our own time. In other words, and seen from a perspective of historical discontinuity, present-day sports are no longer the endpoint of one of those long sagas of progress or decay that we have all read so many times. For to understand the tradition behind most sports today, we indeed need go back no further than the early nineteenth century.

This gap between the athletic worlds of the more remote past and the beginning of our own athletic tradition should be kept in mind while reading the series of brief sketches that follow. These sketches of Greek, Roman, medieval, and Renaissance "sports" are idiosyncratic in that they concentrate on several themes crucial to my search for a way to adequately praise athletic beauty. And also because they do not take up sports outside the European tradition. While it would be fascinating to understand better those athletic-looking choreographies that were attached to rituals of human sacrifice in some precolonial South American cultures, we have more than enough to do in rethinking sports within our own Western tradition. Following these scenes from isolated worlds in the past, I will go on to narrate the emergence of modern sports since the early nineteenth century as a continuous (but certainly not linear) development. This avalanche-like process shows few signs of slowing down in the twenty-first century.

In the past as well as the present, texts that speak

about sports hardly ever describe them in their physical reality, while there is no shortage of documents about the organization and social control of athletics. Quite literally, we cannot even be sure what certain sports of the past may have looked like. Most books and essays about sports history overflow with biographical anecdotes or chronological data, but they rarely offer materials or even suggestions for our visual imagination. At the same time, many authorities in this field seem to be obsessed with proving (and denouncing) the use of sports for nonathletic purposes and functions. If I do not engage in this kind of critique, it is frankly because I do not see a realistic alternative to what it mainly accuses. All historical institutions have been "used" by other institutions and have left their traces on them. In the early nineteenth century, for example, athletics suddenly became a central dimension of England's education system and in the process ended up establishing fairness as an ethical value. This type of appropriation is simply how institutions function—and why should we complain about it? Sports are no exception, except perhaps in that we think they somehow ought to be exceptional.

Demigods

IF YOU TAKE A CAR from Athens to the Isthmus of Corinth, and then drive across the winding mountain roads of the Peloponnese Peninsula to the distant village of Olympia, some thirty miles inland from the Ionian Sea, you will soon begin to feel what a commitment it was to walk or travel on horseback to the ancient Olympic games. Yet hundreds of athletes and tens of thousands of spectators, protected by an Olympics truce, made the journey every four years, over the span of a millennium or more—from 776 BC to 394 AD (the conventionally accepted dates of the ancient Olympic games). As you try to imagine this bodily effort, for which there is simply no equivalent in the modern world, you may begin to wonder what the specific attraction of those five days spent at Zeus' most famous sanctuary could have been.

One answer, a modern answer but valid nevertheless, comes when you arrive at this shady green valley, where the Kladeos and Alpheios rivers join under lush foliage, a place so different from the arid stony landscape through which you have traveled, with growing impatience, during several hours. For ancient guests who had walked for days and even weeks, this contrast upon arrival must have triggered intense feelings of sensual pleasure and relief. Unlike modern tourists, who have the luxury of returning to their air-conditioned hotel rooms for the night, the crowds in ancient Olympia (all men, except for the priestess of Demeter and her maidens) endured narrow quarters, a shortage of water, and blistering heat. And yet their lives held nothing more glorious or more desirable than being precisely there, in that place, to watch athletes compete.

Olympia was just one of the traditional places, along with Delphi, Isthmia, and Nemea, where free men from the various Greek states and colonies came together for panhellenic games, but it was the oldest and most charismatic site. So outstanding was Olympia's fame that the four-year rhythm of its games became the most widely accepted measure for marking time in ancient Greece. Each Olympiad (four-year period) was named for the winner in the first athletic event of the five-day competition. Unlike the spectators (and also the artists, musicians, and orators who came to showcase their talents on the margins of sporting events), athletes spent at least a month before the games at Elis, thirty-five miles from Olympia, where they trained to reach the peak of physical conditioning.

The five days of the Olympic festival were organized as a complex sequence of athletic events and religious rituals (though we miss the specific appeal of Olympia if we insist too much on the distinction between the two). The first day was dedicated to heralds, musicians, and athletic competitions for adolescents. The second day featured horse races, chariot races (including chariots drawn by mules), and, in the U-shaped 200-yard-long stadium, the core event—the pentathlon, consisting of a foot race, long jump, discus, javelin, and wrestling. All stadion races that were not part of the pentathlon took place on the third day. The fourth day was devoted to wrestling, boxing, and the pankration (a very aggressive, almost sadistic type of wrestling or kick boxing), mostly taking place at the palestra, a rectangular court surrounded by arcades. Back at the stadium finally, spectators could enjoy the hoplite run, a middle distance race for men in full armor.

Athletes in the panhellenic games performed naked, and since nakedness only became a condition several centuries after this athletic tradition began, we know that performing naked was a cultural rule, not a symptom of an archaic state of society. Before competitions, athletes would spread oil all over their skin, and some historians have explained this practice as a competitive strategy, especially for the wrestling contest, or as a performance enhancement. I am not convinced that strategic advantage was the most important reason, however. The oil made the naked bodies of athletes glisten with reflected sunlight, and this very palpable aura set them apart from ordinary men.

Aside from the nakedness of athletes, the most surprising features of this program from a modern fan's perspective are the complete absence of team sports and also the rule that the owners of horses, mules, and chariots could be among the Olympic winners. Much less surprising is the obvious reference to military skills. It makes us understand how unheard of any distinction between athletic events and other types of bodily performance in everyday life would have been within Greek culture. Greek spectators thus followed and appreciated most of the competitions as experts, based on knowledge gained from their daily experience.

Among the religious rituals performed at Olympia, the most important were the sacrifice for the dead on the second day, the sacrifice to Zeus followed by a meal for all athletes on the third day, and the closing banquet that came after the proclamation of the victors on the fifth day. Pindar's *Ode on Theron of Acragas* attempted to capture these final moments of boundless joy and pride, and make them resonate with a glory that only the gods can bestow:

> . . . Winning
> releases from anxieties one who engages in
>   competition.
> Truly, wealth embellished with virtues
>   provides fit occasion for various
>   achievements
> by supporting a profound and questing
>   ambition;
> it is a conspicuous lodestar, the truest
>   light for man . . .

Pindar's odes, with their (for us, obsessive) focus on the joy and pride that came with athletic triumphs, suggest several answers to our question about what attracted spectators and athletes alike to the panhellenic games. I believe the appeal for spectators was, first of all, being in the presence—in the physical presence—of the athletes' shining bodies at the moment of their highest performance. The spectator's role as witness to greatness was intensified by the fact that the Olympic games were an extremely high-stakes competition. In no other Western culture has winning been as crucial as it was in ancient Greece. Only the victor earned the right to wear the garland of wild olive. Any consolation for being second best was unknown—there was no equivalent to our silver or bronze medals, there were no records kept of athletes' individual achievements. The same winner-take-all attitude was true, by the way, for many nonathletic institutions in ancient Greece, such as inventing and staging tragedies or comedies at Athens (which took place as a competition between different playwrights) and public speaking (guilt or innocence in Greek trials, for example, was ultimately decided on the basis of oratorical excellence). Winning and being remembered at Olympia gave athletes, their families, and their towns bragging rights that they used with a shamelessness we find hard to reconcile with our idealized view of ancient Greek culture.

For the athletes themselves, there were also more practical payoffs. Alkibiades, otherwise known to us from Plato's *Dialogues* as a beautiful young man and an admirer of Socrates, drew a straight line from his Olympic triumphs to claims of political influence: "I entered seven chariots, a number that no private citizen had ever entered before, and won the first prize and the second and the fourth [meaning three first prizes], and provided everything else in a style worthy of my victory. For by general custom such things do indeed mean honor and from what is done, men infer power." The greatest privilege offered to an Olympic victor— the right to have a statue of his body sculpted and exhibited within the Olympic precinct—was so highly valued by Greeks that the athlete's hometown often sustained its winners with a lifelong pension. Since winning at the panhellenic games provided quite a number of athletes with such permanent sources of income, we can say that a particular version of professionalism had emerged long before the ideal of the "amateur" in the modern Olympic tradition.

But above all, as Pindar's hymn makes clear, being in the immediate presence of athletic greatness at Olympia meant being close to the gods. Unlike the omnipresent and mostly immaterial monotheistic God whose overpowering attributes are so familiar to us, Greek gods inhabited specific places in the world, with greater or lesser intensity, long before they began to take on various human (and nonhuman) incarnations. To be at Olympia was to be in the presence of Zeus himself. And yet I think it is too one-sided to imagine that the panhellenic games were essentially religious events. For it is just as plausible to turn all this around and view Greek gods as the divine incarnation of athletes. In the Greek imagination, gods were fast and mighty, erotically potent and irresistibly appealing, eternally drunk or insuperably alert, overwhelmingly beautiful or repulsively ugly. Sporting such hyperbolic features, they were endlessly competitive with one another, just like their human counterparts. This competitive drive of both gods and men is what the *Iliad* highlights and celebrates more than any other dimension. Homer represented the epic fights between Achilles and Hector, Agamemnon and Priam, Greeks and Trojans not just as human conflicts but as enactments of a divinely competitive spirit.

Because the boundaries that separated Greek gods from humans were so permeable, to aim for the highest level of physical perfection and to win an Olympic competition indeed elevated the victor to the status of a demigod (the ancient meaning of "hero" is "demigod"). For spectators at this event, being in a place where divine and heroic presence converged through athletes' performance, in an uncannily beautiful landscape, was the most ecstatic and transcendental experience that their lives had to offer. Those who gathered at Zeus' Olympic sanctuary must have felt not just well but boundlessly well—about themselves, about the athletes, and about the divinely-infused world of which they were so intimately a part. Every four years, for a short span of time in this very specific place, religious ecstasy and athletic ecstasy became one.

Gladiators

ALTHOUGH THE RUINS of the Colosseum, which was built in 72 AD under the emperor Vespasian, do not lie in the very center of modern Rome, we can easily imagine how busy and intense its surroundings must have been during imperial times. This stadium was located between the Roman Forum, which continued to be a hub of public political activity, the Domus Aurea (or Golden House), a sumptuous palace erected a decade earlier by Nero, and the Circus Maximus, a giant race track offering space for perhaps 300,000 spectators (we "know" it from the film *Ben Hur,* as we all "know" the Colosseum from *Gladiator*). But the Colosseum itself was, by design, a closed circle of insularity in the midst of all this bustling activity. While the stadion at Olympia was open toward the Temple of Zeus and the other athletic facilities within the sanctuary, the Colosseum's free-standing, perfect circle (made possible by the strength of Roman concrete) imposed a separation from its environment, much as most modern stadiums do.

Between sixty thousand and seventy thousand spectators could be seated inside, separated in different sections according to their social status, with the emperor's box being the primary focus of reference for events that unfolded in the arena. The Colosseum featured a subterranean system of corridors, pulleys, and trapdoors through which gladiators, animals, and props could emerge to the surface, and a velarium—a system of sail-like awnings rigged on ropes, manned by sailors—to protect the audience from sun and rain. On hot days, perfumed water may have been sprinkled onto the masses assembled in the Colosseum.

Unlike the Olympic stadion, the Colosseum did not have a pre-established, recurrent schedule of events. The organization of games depended on the generosity and political interests of sponsors, mostly members of the imperial household or wealthy citizens. Financing games at the Colosseum was a means to gain the sympathy of crowds for political purposes, and there seems to have been no embarrassment attached to that fact. The famous slogan "bread and circuses" *(panem et circenses)* described the situation accurately. Once a sponsor decided to offer games in the Colosseum, he would hire an entrepreneur (called an "editor") who specialized in the organization of mass spectacles—what we today might call an event planner. The editor would put together a program that lasted for several days (the longest sequence of this kind, in the early second century AD, went for 123 days), and he advertised his program with written handouts and heralds throughout the capital.

A day at the Colosseum typically featured a variety of shows (all of them accompanied by music), ranging from athletic events in the Greek style and simulated hunts for exotic animals to the main event—combats between individual gladiators or between large teams of gladiators. In addition to their renowned passion for chariot races, Roman crowds developed a liking for the reenactment of historical battles, particularly naval battles, which required removal of the floor and flooding of the arena. While grisly executions were not uncommon, modern research has cast doubt on the notion that Christians or other religious dissenters were routinely put to death for the entertainment of spectators.

Although most gladiators were slaves who lived and practiced in barracklike quarters next to the Colosseum, a good number were free citizens. And even a slave, if he won several battles, could expect to receive a handsome income, which he might invest in buying his citizenship. The win-loss record of each individual gladiator was announced as he appeared in the arena, suggesting that an aura comparable to present-day athletic stardom existed in this brutal world. A high level of athletic skills (identical to the military skills of the period) was required to survive; but in contrast to our modern idea of fair play, in the arena, as in a real battle, the notion of a level playing field did not exist. In the first place, gladiators arrived with endlessly varied types of equipment. A standard foot soldier, with his spear and shield, was often pitted against a *thraex,* who had a smaller shield and a scimitar. A *retiarius,* armed with a trident and a net, was paired with a *pontarius,* whose weapons were adapted to battling from an elevated position. There were *secutores, scissores, provocatores, sagittarii,* and many other roles, names, and types of equipment. The only principle consistently followed in the pairing of gladiators seems to have been that of asymmetry between the fighters. Not only were opponents outfitted with different equipment, but they were hardly ever balanced in

the effectiveness of their weapons, the protective-
ness of their armor, or even their sheer physical
strength.

Unlike many other Roman philosophers and
writers, Seneca, who died a few years before the
construction of the Colosseum, was not fond of
gladiator games. For him, the fact that many
wealthy Romans invested considerable money and
passion into the success of a state-of-the art stable
of fighters was a symptom of an ethical crisis in
the empire. Seneca came close to the average intellectual view of our times in describing gladiators'
combats as "sheer murder" which catered to the
lowest instincts of the crowds. Astonishingly, however, he overlooked a different and very central fascination that gladiator games held for Romans, a
fascination with a striking affinity to certain motifs
of his own stoic philosophy.

Seneca was well able to see this affinity when he
used gladiator games as metaphors for human existence. But he seems to have been blind to it whenever gladiator games themselves stood in the center
of his argument. The fascination he overlooked,
and which many other authors (among them
Cicero and even some of the Church fathers) saw,

focused on what Romans called "the moment of truth," that is, the moment when one of the fighters had lost the contest and faced death in public. We all are familiar, from so many Hollywood films, with the iconic scene in which the emperor decides whether a defeated gladiator will be allowed to survive or will receive a lethal blow from his opponent. This ritual was a historical reality, although the emperor's gesture was not a thumbs-down or thumbs-up. But counter to the movie version and to Seneca's prejudice, statistical research shows that the vast majority of combats (the proportion may have been 10:1) ended with the release of the conquered fighter.

If then it was not the crowd's bloodlust to which the sponsors catered, what can possibly have been the appeal of this ritualized scene whose form was there to stage the imminence of death and extend its agonizing duration? Together with the initial asymmetry between the combatants, the moment of truth must have drawn the crowd's attention exclusively toward not the victor but the loser, who—for a few moments at least—lived publicly in the face of death. What the conquered fighter was expected to show under this trying circumstance was composure, a face "frozen as ice," "hard as stone," impenetrable as a mask. *Mask* is believed to have been the original meaning of the Latin word *persona*, and it is not too far-fetched to imagine that, for Roman culture, it was such face-saving in the presence of potential personal destruction that would shape and indeed make a "person." In this interpretation of gladiator games, the actual combat, with its inherent unfairness, was just the opening act—a precondition for the production of the moment of truth. Showing composure in the face of such grave uncertainty could transfigure the defeated gladiator into the true hero of the spectacle—not a hero as demigod but a hero as icon for the psychic strength required to brave human frailty. Such a source of fascination probably was not part of the average Roman spectator's consciousness, but it must have increased the intensity of his experience nevertheless.

From a modern point of view, this thesis (which seems to be widely accepted among present-day specialists of Roman cultural history) will not quite transform the spectacles of the Colosseum into the humane rituals that we often imagine the ancient Olympic games to have been. Nevertheless, by assigning the role of central protagonist to the conquered gladiator rather than to the winner and by highlighting the choreographed conflict between agony and self-control, this reinterpretation of gladiator games helps us to imagine how Romans must have viewed their existence and survival. The best a citizen could do in that uncertain world was bear his own suffering with stoical composure.

Knights

HARDLY ANY OTHER PERIOD of Western history offered more adverse conditions for the emergence of athletic events than the Middle Ages. A culture in which the all-powerful Church required humans to serve God through their labor six days of the week and to praise Him on Sunday did not leave much time or psychological space for the growth of games and sports. In addition, physical exercise, effort, and pain were ubiquitous and unavoidable for members of all social groups, and so were not likely to become objects of desire. For these reasons and others, the descriptions we have of knightly tournaments—the one ritual in medieval culture that seems to suggest an affinity with sports—may well be nothing but a product of protoliterary imagination. We may never know whether tournaments similar to those narrated by the courtly romances of the twelfth and thirteenth centuries took place in real medieval life. If we do want to argue that those literary scenes are indicative of something similar to athletic practice, then I believe we must adopt the angle of looking at medieval courtly culture as a counterculture, removed from the mainstream of daily life as most medieval men and women experienced it.

The love songs that we call troubadour poetry are the earliest manifestations of this courtly counterculture, and the historical protagonist canonized as the first troubadour is William IX of Aquitaine, a feudal lord in southwestern France who was born in 1071 and died in 1127. William spent his entire life in conflict with the theological authority and political power of the Catholic clergy. While he ultimately lost this uneven battle, he was remarkable and perhaps even unique in reacting to measures of clerical repression with multiple gestures of provocation—gestures that contemporary historians recorded with outward disapproval and secret sympathy. This must be the reason why William's name became attached to a small number of songs that speak about erotic prowess and adulterous relationships in unequivocal words. One of these songs narrates the story of a nobleman who, disguised as a pilgrim and pretending to be mute, has two ladies invite him to their chamber, where they have sex "for eight days, one hundred and eighty-eight times," to the point of complete (male) exhaustion—at which point the ladies reactivate the false pilgrim's energies by dragging the claws of a red cat down his back.

Despite William's impressive, indeed record-breaking, stats, I do not propose to interpret his double-layered physical performance (bringing together the singing of songs and insuperable erotic prowess) as a medieval equivalent of sports. What I want to highlight, rather, is the distance of courtly culture from ethical seriousness and clerical control. This distance was the structural equivalent of the autonomy that surrounds modern art. And such a countercultural perspective may indeed be the angle we need to assume if we want to understand and appreciate those beautiful descriptions of knightly tournaments in the romances that Chrétien de Troyes, the supposed author of the earliest known versions of the King Arthur legend, invented many decades after William IX's exploits.

Chrétien's literary description of Lancelot winning joust after joust under the eyes and in honor of Guinèvere, his lady and King Arthur's adulterous wife, makes clear that those who read his texts or listened to their recitation were at least dreaming of an environment where physical strength and military skill could be transfigured, through the passion of love, into what would have been an equivalent of sports:

> While the Queen was out of the country, I think the remaining young ladies took counsel among themselves, not knowing what to do. They wanted to get married soon. The decision of the council was to hold a tournament . . . They published the news and had it cried all through the neighboring lands and the distant ones too; long beforehand they had the date of the tournament announced, to draw more people. And the Queen came

back before the chosen date . . . The crowds
assembled, the Queen and all the ladies,
knights, and others. Left and right were
many attendants. At the tourneying-ground
was a large timber grandstand since the
Queen was there and the ladies and maidens;
never was seen such a beautiful one, so large
and so well made . . . The jousters moved off
to their jousting, easily finding partners who
had come for the same; others limbered up
for other knightly exercises. The fields were
so full, and the plowland and the clearings,
that one could not guess the number of
knights, so many were there . . . When Lancelot reached the tournament, he was worth
twenty of their best, and began fighting so
well no one could take their eyes off him,
wherever he rode . . . The Queen drew aside a
discreet and sensible maid and said, "Damsel,
you must take a message, and quickly; it's not
long. Go down from the grandstand to that
knight with the red shield."

Should similar jousts between two individual
knights on horseback have taken place as competitive athletic events, the invested level of strength

and body control must have been extraordinary. Such a confrontation would have required a coordinated combination of speed, aim, timing, force, endurance, and above all balance. And yet in the most interesting descriptions of medieval tournaments, the central role of the event is played by the ladies in the grandstand. They are not only spectators but also prizes offered to the winners. The "joy of the court," as Chrétien de Troyes repeatedly calls it, the joy supposedly triggered by tournaments and other courtly celebrations, may have been a fusion of pride over athletic achievement with anticipation of erotic ecstasy. In addition, it could have had its origin in the participants' excitement over an unusual if temporary freedom snatched from clerical control. Under these specific and exceptional conditions, physical exercise could have truned into a source of joy, even in the medieval world.

But the historical reality of medieval tournaments was probably somewhat less joyful. The few hard facts available to us suggest that during the second half of the twelfth century, aristocratic allies in the northwestern regions of present-day France regularly engaged in friendly battles on horseback. However, the function and style of these exercises must have been more akin to military field practice than to the charming scenes evoked by the literature of those days. What distinguished the structure of those contests from serious warfare was a rule that excluded the use of weapons behind a line drawn on either side of the designated battlefield, and another rule that allowed the conquering knight to keep the horses and armor of his defeated opponents. Both regulations may well have been compatible with real military field practice for all we know. We *do* know that Guillaume le Maréchal, one of the most famous knights among his contemporaries, was able to accumulate a small fortune based on his victories in tournaments. But should we therefore call him a professional athlete? The historians see him simply as a member of the lower nobility who, thanks to exceptional competence, was granted the opportunity to improve his economic and social status by competing in tournaments.

However far a historical protagonist like Guillaume le Maréchal may have been from the status of an athlete, since the thirteenth century the memory of knightly tournaments—perhaps the false memory of rituals that never existed—began to inform and to enhance a nostalgic passion, above all in the now-emerging cities, for staged tournaments in the form of expensive, abundant, and increasingly sophisticated pageantry. The shining armor that today occupies considerable space in so many European and even American museums was produced for these pageants. It never had any military function, and it certainly was much too heavy to allow for any form of athletic competition. On some rare occasions, however, the nostalgic imagination of the Late Middle Ages turned what was basically choreographed pageantry into events of a slightly more competitive physical reality. We know of some so-called knights (mostly in Spain and France during the fourteenth and fifteenth centuries) who publicly announced they would "defend" a chosen bridge or a gate against all challengers, mostly in honor of a lady—and these knights, strangely enough, ended up engaging in real jousts with other knights who playfully challenged them.

Perhaps there was even a remote affinity between this obsession with defending bridges and gates and the supposed origin of a game called *jeu de paume* that some sports historians have identified as the predecessor of tennis. Its first players may have been monks hitting a ball with their palms (hence the name "game of palm") against an arch in their cloisters, while other monks "defended" this gate.

Ruffians

THE DOUBLING of imagined (or real) competitions with choreographies that copied the basic forms of competition but did not allow for actual physical confrontation recurred with regularity into the early modern period. Most of what we subsume today under the vague concept of pageantry was the result of this doubling. Although we cannot trace an uninterrupted institutional continuity that would connect the structures of such games to present-day team sports, certain features of our team sports seem to have appeared for the first time in this context.

A typical case is the game of *calcio,* which was popular among Florentine aristocrats during the

Medici centuries. It was played on the piazzas of Florence during carnival season by two teams of twenty-seven men. Eventually the event diverged into a competitive version *(calcio diviso)* and a pageantry version *(calcio a livrea),* both of which probably had a certain resemblance to present-day rugby. At least this is what Florentine texts suggest, in astonishing descriptive detail: "Once he had caught the ball with his hands, he was running along the field with such force and such speed that whoever had the privilege of watching this precious young man was in awe: And then he kicked the ball with such power that it came down just one arm away from the goal line."

While the game of *calcio* was a pastime and source of entertainment for noblemen and other wealthy participants, there were related forms of physical competition (some involving the defense and press of bridges or gates) where each team represented a specific neighborhood, social group, or craft. The objective always was to collectively run and literally ram an equivalent of today's soccer or rugby ball toward a goal, against the physical resistance of another group of male bodies. Instead of actively engaging in these more violent competitions, many aristocrats served as patrons of teams or of individual athletes—and they also bet serious amounts of money on their champions.

The ambivalent role of aristocratic spectators to these ruffian games, whose disinterested admiration for players' performances must have sometimes conflicted with their often substantial financial stake in the outcome, would become the condition for the emergence of boxing in England as the first fully developed professional sport of the modern era (and the one significant exception to the thesis that modern sports did not begin before the early nineteenth century). The eighteenth-century version of boxing was incomparably more brutal than even the most aggressive professional matches today. Fighters hit and defended themselves with bare knuckles, and cuts and injuries of their hands often became the reason for defeat. Above all, matches ended only with a decisive knock-out or the complete exhaustion of one fighter (and sometimes even both fighters). Contests lasting more than fifty rounds and many hours were not unusual. A large archive of pictures from this period present in grueling detail the consequences of those long fights. And yet the social and cultural similarities with the world of present-day boxing are striking.

Since its modern beginnings, boxing has held a particular fascination for people at both extremes of the social spectrum—for the wealthy and cultivated as well as criminals and outcasts. And since its inception, modern boxing has been the object of all kinds of illegal manipulation. To this day, one can never know for sure whether a fight has been fixed—and this uncertainty, strangely enough, contributes to boxing's fascination. Images from the early years of modern boxing reflect such tensions and ambiguities in amazing detail, capturing for our imagination the social and spatial vicinity where boxing, prostitution, and crime come together with such explosive energy. They highlight the contrast between different social ranks of spectators, all of whom clearly relished the beaten and bleeding bodies at the end of the fight more than the immaculate contestants at the beginning.

Boxing has also inspired an almost irresistible urge among spectators to practice the sport themselves. The "gentleman boxer" with his intellectual touch was already a fully developed type in the first century of boxing. Its first incarnation was Jem

Belcher, who held the heavyweight title at several intervals in the early nineteenth century. According to Pierce Egan's *Boxiana* from 1813:

> Belcher had a prepossessing appearance, genteel, and remarkably placid in his behaviour. There was nothing that indicated superior bodily strength; yet, when stripped, his form was muscular and elegant. The science that he was master of, appeared exclusively his own—and his antagonists were not aware of the singular advantages that it gave him over those who studied and fought upon the accustomed principles of pugilism; its was completely intuitive; practice had rendered its effects powerful, and in confusing his antagonists he gained considerable time to improve his native advantage with promptitude and decision . . . In his social hours JEM was good-natured, and modest and unassuming. In the character of a publican no man entertained a better sense of propriety and decorum than Belcher did.

It is interesting how moral qualities, which in this text and others go together with the fighter's physical prowess, resemble the virtues that Roman spectators saw in their gladiators. From the beginning of modern boxing, the defeats and tragedies of the great protagonists fascinated fans much more than their victories. Jem Belcher turned out to be no exception. After retiring early and losing an eye in a non-sports-related accident, he tried to come back but was decisively beaten. His fans, however, seem to have experienced Belcher's last fight as his finest hour: "Yet, notwithstanding the spectators perceived a deficiency in Belcher's fighting in several parts, from his not being able to guard off the attacks as heretofore, and the severe punishment which his head and face had sustained in the combat; his afflicting situation made a deep impression, not only upon his friends, but the company in general, and the involuntary tear was seen silently stealing down the iron cheek of many present, for the loss of departing greatness in their favorite hero."

Being mainly organized as open-air events, some of the great boxing matches in London during the early nineteenth century attracted crowds between twenty thousand and thirty thousand spectators. These numbers confirm that, on many different levels, the development of boxing anticipated the arrival of other modern sports by a good century.

Sportsmen

AMONG MORE CULTIVATED
boxing fans in the eighteenth century, a main explanation for their fascination with this brutal contest may have been the rubber-band effect—a reaction to the insistence of Enlightenment culture on
the priority of mind and reason over body and
senses. Sports movements of the nineteenth century often looked for legitimation to the biographies and books of authors who, even during the
Enlightenment, had expressed a desire to return to
more sensual aspects of life. One of these was
Johann Wolfgang von Goethe, who considered
regular physical exercise, above all swimming and
skating, as a necessary condition for keeping his
own wit and productivity as a writer at their peak.
Another was Jean-Jacques Rousseau, who claimed
to actively enjoy the authenticity of untouched
nature and whose pedagogical treatise *Emile* embraced physical education. That many famous
mountains of the Alps were climbed for the first
time by well-to-do young gentlemen during the
late eighteenth century can be read as an early sig-

nal of a cultural shift in the direction of the senses and bodily experience.

But it was only in the early nineteenth century that the desire to return to nature and to redress the imbalance between body and mind found a social context for the growth of what we would call modern sports. As a consequence of revolutions and reforms during the previous century, leisure time—once a privilege of the upper classes—became a promise made to all citizens. At a time when many other of the new states' social promises went unfulfilled, leisure and leisure-time activities took on a mediating function by allowing members of the middle class to believe they had become what they had always wanted (and had been promised) to be—equal members of society, free in the choice of professions and roles and, above all, successful independent of their social origin. The occasional satisfaction of a pre-Romantic desire (the Lord is nostalgic, travels to Switzerland, admires the Matterhorn) became progressively transformed into institutionalized practice, based on rules and well-described skills that allowed for much larger participation—and into an increasingly clear perception of a distance between this practice and the everyday sphere of labor and work (members of a mountaineering club, during their annual vacation, travel jointly to the French Alps to climb Mont Blanc).

Also in the nineteenth century, leisurely activities became central components in emerging programs of national and individual education. In Germany, particularly in Prussia, this development took a practical and disciplinarian turn. Friedrich Ludwig Jahn invented the program of gymnastics in Berlin with the explicit goal of strengthening German youth for the wars of liberation against Napoleon. The horse as a gymnastic event, for example, has thus a very real historical and political origin. A rigid form and a paramilitary function for every movement, together with the hope of returning to the imagined strength of German ancestors, were core elements in the participants' commitment. *Turnen,* the word that Jahn invented for his new sport, was meant to bring back the sounds of an archaic Germanic language.

In the larger European and North American context, Jahn's contribution to modern sports was considered eccentric (and fortunately so, one feels compelled to add). More popular and successful than gymnastics were boxing, wrestling, fencing, tennis and golf, horse racing and boat racing, mountaineering and hiking. All of these activities had existed before the nineteenth century, of course, but they were now embraced by more adolescents with greater energy, conviction, and expectation than ever before. No institution was more instrumental in this process than British schools and universities. Inspired by German intellectuals like the archaeologist Johann Joachim Winckelmann and the poet Friedrich Hölderlin, who in the eighteenth and early nineteenth centuries had rediscovered and appropriated ancient Greek body culture, British schools made this imagined ideal the model for educating cosmopolitan English gentlemen. Anticipating the concept of amateurism, the universities of Oxford and Cambridge did not allow professional boatsmen to participate in the first race between their crew teams in 1829. By 1859 this rowing contest was held on an annual basis. Other team sports also enjoyed growing popularity among British students. Cricket, after existing as a gentlemanly game throughout the eighteenth century, made its way into the universities around this time. Early and not yet clearly differentiated forms of rugby and soccer emerged.

Pedagogues hailed the new team sports in particular as a medium for the promotion of a new social ethos that was acquiring the name of "sportsmanship." It was supposed to bring together a commitment to one's own team with respect for and fairness toward one's opponent. This was one basis for the much quoted proverb of the "healthy mind in a healthy body" *(mens sana in corpore sano),* which had never had a similar valence during classical antiquity. Meanwhile, without ever softening the shrill patriotic tones of its early years, German *Turnen* developed into a mass movement more closely affiliated with political powers promoting a German nation-state than with physical education in school programs. By mid-nineteenth century, the annual Turnfeste had become a powerful expression of German nationalism, attracting up to thirty thousand participants.

In the English-speaking countries, professional sports like horse racing and boxing, with their associated betting fever, drew large crowds and remained unperturbed by the emerging amateur sporting ethos. Running events in track and field were also still part of the world of professionalism (and betting) under the name of pedestrian sports, rather than being integrated into the growing movement of college athletics. Baseball, by contrast, was neither professional nor academic during its early history, and perhaps this is one of the factors that made it so particularly American. Despite the strangely stubborn desire of many baseball enthusiasts of our time to invent a rural (if not bucolic) past for their favorite game, the foundation of the first baseball club could not have happened in more metropolitan, middle-class surroundings.

On September 23, 1845, a group of young gentlemen from New York who, since the spring of 1842, had met each weekend to play ball at the corner of Madison Avenue and 27th Street established themselves as the New York Knickerbocker Base Ball Club. Soon they began to take the ferry across the Hudson River to Hoboken, New Jersey, once or twice a week, where they played in a grassy picnic grove called by the most fitting of names, Elysian Field. The Knickerbockers' first president was a physician, and their constitution declared that they played for "health and recreation merely." But the flavor of the gatherings seems to have been somewhat less spiritual and idealistic. During the early years of the club, Knickerbocker games were regularly followed by champagne suppers.

By 1869 the all-leisure, all-bourgeois era of baseball had come to an end, crowded out by both college and professional teams. Ten years earlier, two western Massachusetts schools, Amherst and Williams, faced each other in the first intercollegiate baseball game, inaugurating the entry of America's soon-to-be-favorite pastime into the high-energy world of college athletics. Then in 1869 a group of Ohio investors financed the first professional baseball team, the Cincinnati Red Stockings, and hired Harry Wright, the British-born son of a professional cricketer, to manage them. On St. Patrick's Day, 1871, the National Association of Professional Base Ball Players declared its independence from the older baseball association whose mission had been to keep alive the gentlemen's version of the game. A professional league of nine teams was formed, of which three franchises, the Boston Red Stockings, the Chicago White Stockings, and the Philadelphia Athletics (now the Oakland A's), still play in the major leagues today. By 1876 the first financial crisis hit professional baseball, giving owners a welcome opportunity to reduce salaries to $800, declaring that it was "ridiculous to pay ballplayers $2,000 a year."

The simultaneous emergence of leisure, college, and professional sports motivated the founding of national (and soon also international) sports associations, whose greatest achievement was to establish the rules and regulations of play. This homogenization went together with a process of differentiation, above all in England, between games that allowed players to secure the ball with their hands (and to defend it from some style of aggressive tackling) and other versions that excluded handling the ball (and reduced the likelihood of vicious body attacks). This differentiation would eventually create rugby (which in American colleges became football) and association football (known in the United States as soccer). Such rapid diversification between more violent and more fluid forms of ballgames reflects a revolution in taste for which nobody has found a convincing explanation yet.

The Football Association of England, founded

in 1863, continued to refine and stabilize the game in subsequent editions of its rulebook until it reached an (almost) final version in 1892. Since then, soccer has been very similar to the game we know today, except of course for the higher level of physical performance and the larger crowds. Photographs from the earliest days of professional soccer give the impression that it was once a game for a few lonesome enthusiasts. But by 1888 the Football Association represented a professional league whose games followed Association rules and whose players were recruited mainly among young factory workers. The Fédération Internationale de Football Association (FIFA) was established at Paris in 1904, at a time when national soccer organizations were fast emerging all over Europe. Doubtless because of the unique popularity of college and university sports in the United States, a corresponding divergence between amateur and professional football got under way much later, in the 1920s. And not until the third quarter of the twentieth century was professional football able to mount any kind of serious competition with college football for the hearts and minds of fans.

Olympians

AMATEUR SPORTS REACHED its apotheosis in the modern Olympic movement. This triumph of organized amateurism was the almost single-handed achievement of Pierre Frédy, Baron de Coubertin, a well-read French aristocrat with an astonishing flair for diplomacy. Born in 1863, Coubertin grew up in a nation struggling with the trauma of defeat in its war against Prussia, a defeat that led to both the collapse of the Second French Empire and the foundation of the Second German Empire. Yet Coubertin did not seem to worry much about rising German nationalism or the formidable German *Turner.* Displaying an exceptional intellectual generosity, he came to admire the achievements of German classicists and archaeologists whose excavations had brought to light the ruins of ancient Olympia. But hailing the conquests of contemporary archaeology was one thing; reaching a historically adequate understanding of ancient athletics turned out to be quite another.

Coubertin identified the panhellenic games with amateurism and with an attitude that valued mere participation more highly than winning. Both of these misreadings of the ancient Olympics would shape modern sports decisively. But we should not overdramatize the consequences of Coubertin's misinterpretation. Even without his Olympic ideology, an equivalent concept of amateurism would probably have emerged in reaction to the expansion of professional sports. Evidence of this comes from the long-forgotten workers' olympiads initiated by the Soviet Union after the October revolution of 1917. Like Coubertin's initiative, the workers' sports movement was officially both antinationalist and antiprofessional (though it took care to differentiate itself from Coubertin's heavily bourgeois, even aristocratic, Olympic organization).

Thanks perhaps to his aristocratic preference for horseback riding and fencing (along with the very French addition of bicycle racing), the founder of the modern Olympic movement felt irresistibly attracted to the values and style of British college sports. But the British responded coolly to Coubertin's proposal to have a French team participate in the annual boat race between Oxford and Cambridge, and British internationalism as Coubertin imagined it turned out to be an illusion. Artistocrats and members of the upper middle class in other parts of Europe and Northern America greeted Coubertin's enthusiasm more warmly. His distaste for nationalism and for the showmanship of professional sports resonated with their own values, and after his presentation on international amateurism at a congress in Paris during the summer of 1894, events developed so quickly that they threatened to escape Coubertin's control. Trying to improve upon his proposal to hold the first modern Olympic games in Paris during the 1900 World's Fair, the Greek delegation launched the idea of holding the inaugural games in Athens during Easter week of 1896. Not to be outdone on the diplomatic front, Coubertin immediately embraced as his own the idea of bringing the Olympic games "back" to Greece.

To everybody's astonishment, he was successful in persuading the Greek royal family to endorse the plan as well, despite the catastrophic state of the nation's finances. At the last minute, a patriotic millionaire came forward with a donation which made the construction of a futuristic stadium possible. It was built on a site in Athens where the ruins of an ancient stadion had been recently excavated, and its outline and many interior architectural details copied what appeared to have been the ancient tradition. But its capacity of seventy thousand seats—unheard of since the days of ancient Rome—made this the first truly modern stadium. From a historical point of view, its opening may well be seen as the most important event of the first modern Olympic games.

Photographs showing huge crowds in attendance at the inaugural celebration, during the arrival of the marathon runners, and for the closing ceremonies (in a city of only two hundred thousand people) make us easily forget that the athletic events themselves were hastily put together, and the performances of the first Olympians were unimpressive even for their time. Invitations to the various national Olympic Committees, most of which were still embryonic, went out very late, and the invited countries faced financial and logistical problems in sending competitors to Athens. Despite Coubertin's central role in this venture, no institution or individual in France felt compelled to sponsor French athletes (rumor has it that the French bicycle racers who won Olympic honors just happened to be in Greece on professional business). The arrival of the American delegation —mostly students from Princeton and Harvard— had been facilitated by a last-minute decision of William Sloane, a friend of Coubertin and a professor at Princeton, to cancel his own and his wife's passage to Athens so that he could donate the money to an anonymous fund that was financing the American team's voyage. Unfortunately (or so I imagine) for the captain of the American track team, Robert Garrett, his widowed mother decided to replace Sloane as the chaperone for her son and his friends.

The twenty-one German participants received support from the imperial family (who wanted to honor their Greek brethren), but upon their return they faced a lifelong ban from the anti-internationalist Turnerbund, by far the most powerful athletic organization in Germany. Among European governments, Hungary showed at least some good intentions toward supporting its delegation at the first Olympics. Considering all these obstacles, it is no wonder that the statistics of participants at the first Olympics looked mediocre. The 262 athletes competing at Athens came from thirteen countries, but only 76 of them were non-Greek.

The athletic events themselves were feats of improvisation, with predictably random results. All crew races, for example, had to be called off due to adverse weather. Under the approving eyes of his mother, Robert Garrett from Princeton won the discus competition although he had never practiced this sport until a few days before. Not unlike Coubertin's homemade Olympic ideology, the program of events looked like a compromise between late-nineteenth-century fantasies about ancient Greece and the obligatory concessions to modern taste. Track and field events, in addition to wrestling, swimming, and perhaps even fencing and weight lifting—that is, sports based on very elementary body movements—were probably chosen to suggest competitive events from the remote past, whereas shooting, cycling, tennis, and (in a gesture of reverence toward Germany) gymnastics and rope climbing must have been seen as more modern components. Remarkably, there were no ballgames at the first Olympics.

The event that, more than any other, embodied the athletic spirit of 1896 was the marathon, invented on uncertain historiographical grounds by Michel Bréal, a philologist and friend of Coubertin. It reenacted a legendary run from a battlefield near the village of Marathon to the city of Athens; the original marathon runner was believed to be a messenger who died upon announcing to the citizens of Athens the 490 BC victory over the Persians. The 1896 event brought together contemporary images of the arid Greek landscape, the historical imagination of the late nineteenth century, and an actual athletic competition. Although the first marathon race of the modern Olympics did not take place on closing day, as it does now, the arrival of the Greek winner, Spiridon Louis, at the modern Olympic stadium in Athens, standing on the site of an ancient Greek stadion, was without a doubt the culminating moment of the games. This is how Burton Holmes, an American visitor and prolific writer of travelogues, saw the winner's triumphant entrance—a fusion of received ideas about ancient Greece and contemporary monarchy:

While from the sloping sides of the Stadium avalanches of applause come crashing down; while the King of Greece so far forgets his royal dignity as to rip the visor from his royal cap in waving it like mad; while staid and proper citizens embrace each other frantically; while tears of joy are shed; while doves, to which long white ribbons are attached, are loosed and flutter in the air; while all Athens utters a triumphant shout, Louis, the simple peasant, the farmer from the little hamlet Amarousi, is escorted by two Princes and a Russian Grand Duke—all three embracing, even kissing him—from the entrance to the far end of the Stadium where he is greeted by a royal hand in the midst of such a scene as Athens has not witnessed in a thousand years.

From today's distant perspective, we can identify the first Athens Olympics as an anticipation of athletics during the first third of the twentieth century. Large crowds in modern stadiums, ever-multiplying international events, and a steadily building tension between amateurism and professionalism—this was the scenario that shaped modern sports between 1896 and the Berlin games of 1936. But from the perspective of those organizing the second and third Olympics, the future success of the games was touch-and-go. Without an increase in spectator fascination, the Olympic movement may not have survived Paris in 1900 or St. Louis in 1904, where its events were marginal sideshows at the then extremely popular world fairs. Not before the 1908 Olympics in London and the 1912 games in Stockholm was the promise embodied by the Athens marathon heartily embraced by international fans.

Subsequent Olympic programs adapted to transformations in politics and taste. Women began to be admitted in 1912, and the popularity of cross-country and downhill skiing led to the first Winter Olympics in 1924. The 1920s exhibited an intense fascination with events that, in one way or other, staged the athletes' confrontation with danger, extreme exhaustion, and death. Those were the golden years of boxing, long-distance running, and alpinism (for which, going back to prior conquests, Olympic medals were awarded in 1936). Above all, ballgames moved to the center of attention, despite being under intense (and well-justified) suspicion of professionalism. Ice hockey, curling, polo, water polo, rugby, and *pelote basque* were on the program for the 1924 Olympics at Chamonix and Paris. But the most popular event in 1924 and again in 1928 at Amsterdam was the soccer tournament, won both times by the "sensational" team from Uruguay, whose elegant and rhythmic playing style inspired all of Europe. The unparalleled success of soccer at these games, and its lingering conflict with the Olympic amateur ideology, led to the creation of a soccer World Cup tournament, which quickly developed into the second largest event in the world of sports. The first tournament took place in Montevideo in 1930, in honor of the hundredth anniversary of Uruguay's independence.

Much, too much perhaps, has been written about the Berlin games that took place six years later, under national-socialist direction. Much has also been said about the now-canonized film by director Leni Riefenstahl which documents the event. So I will take this opportunity to be brief, confining my comments to just two points. First, Hitler's Olympics brought to grotesque perfection the ideology of amateurism, with its idealistic distortions and its over-the-top pageantry. As the introductory sequence of Riefenstahl's film shows (where ancient Greek statues, represented by actors in scarce underwear, morph into live athletes) and as the architecture of the Berlin stadium confirms (featuring a large Marathon Gate as a compromise between the U-shape of the stadion in Olympia and the closed circle of the Colosseum in Rome), nobody had ever gone further in fusing Greek traditions with modern nationalistic claims than the master planners of the Berlin Olympics. A profusely reiterated sequence of ideological equations suggested that modern sports were the sports of ancient Greece, that German culture was the heir of ancient Greek culture, and therefore that sports were both essentially Greek and essentially German.

To embody this triple proposition, Carl Diem, a high school teacher of classics who was Hitler's sports ideologue in charge, invented a new Olympic ritual that has survived to this day and whose claim of archaic authenticity we still want to believe, although it most certainly was never performed before 1936. This is the torch relay of the

Olympic fire which connects the site of Zeus' sanctuary in Olympia with each new Olympic city. In retrospect, we can see that the moment when Germany pushed its Olympic ideology to such an extreme marked the beginning of the end for amateurism. For how serious could the idealized claims and rituals of this cult, with its associated internationalism, be if it lent itself so easily to the interests of a state that embodied the most radical racism and nationalism humankind had ever seen?

The second point is that the Berlin games inaugurated a mutual dependency between sports and communication technology that has increasingly defined our experience as spectators today. The 1936 Olympics not only produced one of the most successful sports films in history, and it not only broadcast full international radio coverage, but it was also the first major event in world history (not only the first athletic event) that was largely covered by television. This fact is so little known because the television pictures taken in the Berlin stadium were screened only in the movie theaters of a few German cities, for handpicked audiences.

What those selected German spectators saw (and what the few of them who are still alive today most vividly remember) was, paradoxically, the breakthrough of African-American athletes to their dominant position in international sports. Most of the still-living spectators particularly recall Jesse's Owens's four explosive victories and the effortless elegance with which he conquered his international competitors. During the postwar years, some people would also "remember" the moment in which, after Owens defeated the German favorite, Lutz Long, in the long jump, the two young men sat down on the lawn of the Olympic stadium and tried to engage in a conversation. But that myth (which I heard from my own father and others endless times) has no documentary basis.

Customers

IF THE TELEVISION broadcast of the Berlin Olympics represented the future of modern sports, what has that future—now our present—become? Let's begin to answer this question by highlighting a statistical fact. During the second half of the twentieth century, practicing sports became a pastime—and even a form of rational behavior—for a larger proportion of the world's population than ever before. The interventions of the health insurance industry helped to elevate physical activity to the status of an ethical and economic obligation. As customers of our insurance companies, we are all summoned to help keep their expenses low by increasing our cardiovascular capacity and lowering our body mass index. So to comply, we join a gym or health club, where, as customers once again, we invest our money in a promise of longevity and professional (not to mention social) success.

Meanwhile, the ideology of amateurism has vanished with hardly a trace. Most top athletes today who are capable of performing on a nationally or internationally competitive level become professionals as soon as possible, sometimes right out of high school. The final step in this economic transformation of sports was taken between the Olympic games of 1984 at Los Angeles and the games of 1988 at Seoul. These were the first Olympics that produced a level of revenue (mostly from TV broadcasting and endorsements) superior to the expenses incurred—a remarkable turnaround, if one considers that the 1976 Olympics at Montreal caused financial problems for the organizing city that are still felt today.

Following the economic success of Olympics broadcasting in the late 1980s, the practical idea emerged that revenue sharing should include athletes whose sports, considered independently, could not produce any income. It is hard to imagine tens of thousands of spectators paying for expensive tickets to see race walkers perform their strangely convoluted movements. But television viewers are a whole different market. Within the cutting-back-and-forth context of a larger track and field broadcast (studded with human interest cameos), race walking can become an engaging sidelight—and a potential inspiration for the hundreds of thousands of viewers who pursue health sports. Television broadcasting, financed by the endorsement industry (which sees every one of those television viewers as a potential customer) has thus developed a feedback relationship between the many millions who practice sports for their own health or recreation and the few thousands who perform sports at a high competitive level. Ironically perhaps, there is reason to think

that many of the overweight early-morning joggers
in Europe or North America carry within them a
self-image shaped by the great Ethiopian distance
runners. If it would still be a slight exaggeration to
say that the life forms of professional athletes and
those of average sports customers are converging,
they are definitely much less neatly separated today
than they were a century ago.

A second development has been less dramatic
than broadcasting, but it must be mentioned in
any picture of present-day sports and their future.
Largely as a result of those economic, political, and
cultural changes that we call globalization, the importance of nationhood in fans' perception of, and
identification with, individual athletes and teams
seems to be receding. It has often been said that
athletes as world-famous as the Williams sisters,
David Beckham, Tiger Woods, or Michael Schumacher have the status of global icons. But could it
also therefore be true that nationality, as an identi-
fier of athletes, is being replaced by the brands
these stars endorse? Has globalization caused athletes to tacitly trade in their national capital for
more individual and purely economic capital? In
some cases this is undeniably happening. World-

wide, Michael Schumacher's image is much more closely tied to the brandname Ferrari than to his native Germany; and for Michael Jordan's hundreds of thousands of fans around the globe, the word Nike may leap to mind more readily when hearing his name than does the word American.

Of course, the duration and stability of the business relations between Nike and Jordan, Ferrari and Schumacher are still exceptions. Far more typical is the soccer star who ends up never being associated with any single brand of footwear because his endorsements change each time he changes teams. But if brand names ever do replace national identities in our perception of famous athletes—if fans become, first and foremost, potential customers for running shoes, cars, and the other accoutrements of athletic stardom—something fundamental in the relationship of fans to their heroes will have shifted.

Looking at sports commercialization another way, I wonder whether a point could ever be reached where sports goes beyond (or perhaps even breaks down) its traditional insularity from the everyday life of sports fans. I refer not to the economic impact of sports but, for example, to the number of hours per week that lawyers, dentists, and engineers in the United States spend on the golf course or at the tennis court, in comparison to the number of hours they invest in their work or volunteer activities or family life. I could certainly berate myself for the time I spend watching sports on television and in the stadium, not to mention my annual expenses for season tickets. But I am not speaking from any specifically moral or political (and even less from a critical or self-critical) standpoint.

Let me try to capture what I find noteworthy through a little allegory from everyday life. A few years ago, when I was taking a group of thirty college students on a field trip to visit traditional Japanese houses in Kyoto, we all followed the Japanese convention of taking off our shoes before entering a private or a religious space. Looking at the pile of Adidas, Nikes, and Reeboks, I realized that I was the only person in that group of thirty-one Americans who was not wearing athletic shoes. Obviously, none of the other thirty people was getting ready to participate in an athletic event, any more than I was. I saw this little social phenomenon as perhaps an indication that sports, in the disguise of leisure culture, may be escaping its conventional bounds and invading the rest of our lives, forcing us into the role of nonstop sports consumers rather than fans.

There are other innovations on the horizon as well. In many sports today, the top athletes have reached a level close to the physical limit of human performance. This is particularly obvious in track and field events, where no breakthroughs comparable to Bob Beamon's long-jump record at the 1968 Olympics have been recorded in recent times, and where the world record for the 100-meter race will certainly never be pushed below nine seconds. As athletes reach the limit of human ability, the issue of drug-enhanced (or even gene-enhanced) performance becomes more salient. Sports that have not shown any immediately plausible limits of performance may continue to resist the use of performance enhancers for awhile. But for other sports, might performance enhancers become just another item in a kit of athletic tools that fans take for granted in competitions, as we do a nine iron or a bobsled? It is not so difficult to think that in a not-so-remote Brave-New-Worldish future, the brandnames of performance enhancers could become attached to the names of famous athletes, just as the names of car manufacturers or shoe producers are today. Will there ever be a world championship for the performance enhancement industry, parallel to the championships that already exist for race car producers? It's not beyond imagining.

While I resist the temptation to judge these questions from a moralistic point of view, the question I find most interesting about the future is also the one that will take us, in the next chapter, to a discussion of sports fascinations. When an ever-increasing number of individual sports reach the limits of human performance, wherever that vanishing point might be, could our interest as fans still be held by the aesthetic appeal of athletes' performances, rather than by quantitative records they will no longer be able to break?

three

FASCINATIONS

W HAT IS IT that fascinates sport spectators, beyond victories, defeats, and broken records? What do they enjoy and, unknowingly perhaps, want to hold onto when they are not focusing on statistics? These questions, which are about the objects of aesthetic experience, are among the decisive questions for a book that wants to praise sports as a source of joy for those who watch them.

Before I attempt an answer, let me bracket some possible topics that one could legitimately associate with spectators' pleasure. By saying that I will not talk about wins, losses, and other records, I might seem to leave open the possibility at least for arete to play a role in producing what we enjoy about sports. But the merits of striving for excellence will not be in the foreground of this chapter. Likewise, I will not return to the structure and acts of aesthetic judgment. For what we enjoy in sports, and what I will discuss as the objects of that experience, belong to a range of phenomena that lie somewhere between performance and the act of judging it. They are body movements always already shaped by the expectations and the appreciation that spectators bring with them to the game.

The in-between status of these body movements makes the word *fascination* my concept of choice. It refers to the eye as attracted to, indeed paralyzed by, the appeal of something perceived (in our case, athletic performance). But it also captures the added dimension that the spectator contributes. All kinds of different dispositions on the spectators' side will contribute to the shaping of different fascinations. If a seasoned gymnastics coach and a novice spectator watch a high bar routine, they both can enjoy what they see, but their fascination will not be the same, simply because their knowledge and engagement are so divergent.

Here, then, are seven different sport fascinations that I will try to describe and supplement with contemporary and historical illustrations: sculpted bodies; suffering in the face of death; grace; tools that enhance the body's potential; embodied forms; plays as epiphanies; and good timing. One specific fascination is often decisive in our enjoyment of a specific event. For example, grace is what we most admire in track and field events, whereas gymnastics is mainly about embodying a set of given forms. Yet there is probably not a single sport whose appeal we can fully grasp by associating it with only one fascination. Several fascinations can, and usually do, come together as we watch individual sports. Long-distance running, in addition to highlighting the grace of competitors, also makes spectators keenly aware of the exhaustion and agony they suffer. During a baseball game we admire the execution of a strategic play at home plate, but we also appreciate the timing involved when a shortstop stretches for a line drive and, in a continuous pivot, throws to first base for a double play.

My typology of fascinations is intended to help us grasp the complex movements we enjoy in watching sports. Beyond that, it contains no unifying principle, no matrix of meanings, no "grammar" to prescribe the ways in which these fascinations can be combined (as intellectuals would have sought at the time when the great Pelé ruled the soccer world). This typology is not, at least not primarily, about representing—and even less about copying—realities. It is about making distinctions among concepts, so that we can name, on a more complex level, exactly what it is we find beautiful about sports. And that may be all there is to the act of praising.

Bodies

LET YOUR IMAGINATION now take you back to the column-surrounded space of an ancient Greek gymnasion, where citizens and their sons went to shape their bodies through exercise and where nakedness was a condition for these workouts. The gymnasion also inspired intellectual conversation, which probably explains why both Plato's Academy and Aristotle's Lyceum grew up next door to a gym. But as we know from Plato's *Dialogues,* intellectual exchange was never separated from the ongoing admiration of beautifully sculpted bodies.

What were the goals of those young (and not so

young) Greek men who spent much time sculpting their bodies, and what limits did they face in achieving these goals? As such questions do not seem to have concerned the Greeks very much, let's try answering them by referring to a workout studio in present-day Los Angeles. If we set aside fitness and health preservation as two perhaps statistically dominant but aesthetically irrelevant motivations for membership in this club, then we are left with two types of body transformation taking place in the gym—and they may have taken place in the ancient gymnasion as well. We can even associate them with the names of two eminent Californians of our time. One modality of body sculpting is embodied by the former Mr. Universe, film star, and present governor of California, Arnold Schwarzenegger. The principle with which we associate Schwarzenegger is the infinite growth of each muscle. Bobybuilders with this orientation (in the best-case scenario) end up looking like anatomical models. But the best anatomical model is not necessarily the one with the largest muscles. It is a shape in which the development of each individual muscle does not spoil but rather enhances a difficult-to-define impression of harmony.

If the Schwarzenegger modality of sculpting one's body involves a gradual progression toward an ideal (an ideal that, strangely, fits Nietzsche's formula of "becoming what you are"), I want to associate the second modality of body sculpting with the name of the philosopher Judith Butler, professor of rhetoric and comparative literature at the University of California, Berkeley. Butler dedicated *Bodies That Matter,* her most influential book, to the question of body transformation. She thinks and writes about body transformation as a slow (and sometimes painful) process based on daily performance. That she also talks about the limits of this process, about the fact that a petite woman who wants to achieve a certain type of athletic body will not always reach this goal, has provoked harsh criticism from Butler's fellow feminists who subscribe to the idea of unlimited gender constructivism—the belief, among other things, that bodies can adapt themselves to any goal of transformation.

The opposite position—the insistence on unavoidable limits—is the point of departure for Butler's pathbreaking aesthetic intuition. Instead of thinking of the goal of body transformation as conforming to shapes that already exist, body sculpting, according to Butler, has the potential of producing an infinity of new and beautifully hybrid forms that move bodies beyond traditional male–female types. Instead of continuing to think about a male type of female body, a woman who is transforming her body by practicing discus throwing or shot-put could enhance and enjoy the discovery of new body forms, forms that are neither female nor male in the conventional sense.

But do the naked male bodies in the Greek gymnasion and the scarcely clad bodies of both sexes in today's workout studios have anything to do with the kind of pleasure that centrally concerns us—the pleasure taken by spectators? The modern workout studio, like the ancient gymnasion, is open only to people who actively engage in exercise themselves, and who are therefore not spectators in the strict sense of the word. On the other hand, ancient athletes and modern bodybuilders share a passion for making their bodies shine through the application of oil and other liquids to their skin, and this practice suggests that bodybuilders think of other bodybuilders as potential spectators. We could say that whoever goes to a gym for a workout is an athlete and a spectator at the same time.

This reflective doubling accounts for the erotically charged atmosphere that has always pervaded the world of body sculpting. It also explains why, since the sixth century BC, the gymnasion became one of those places where Greek men from the upper classes progressed through two stages of homosexual love, first as erotically passive adolescents and later as erotically active young adults. A drinking cup from around 510 BC depicts the courtship of four homosexual couples in a gymnasion. All are wrapped in transparent togas; the four slightly older and slightly taller men embrace the younger men, whose features look delicately prepubescent and whose hairstyles are very elaborate. Three of the older men approach the boys' genitals with their hands. As one of the boys looks up to the lover whose face turns toward him, we sense shyness, trust, and perhaps a spark of awakening passion on the adolescent's face. With his right hand, the boy holds a small flask filled with oil that will make his body shine.

Suffering

NOTHING COULD BE farther from the atmosphere of the ancient Greek gymnasion than a modern boxing ring. If under cover of shyness, caution, and initial restraint the gymnasion aroused and fulfilled erotic desires, the ropes surrounding a boxing ring enclose and barely contain passion of a straightforwardly destructive kind. The devastating consequences of unbridled violence for both athletes and spectators is the second sports fascination I want to explore. Since at least the eighteenth century, boxing has always attracted the cultivated and the wealthy, and yet no spectators have garnered a worse reputation than boxing crowds. The assumption underlying this disrepute is, however, superficial to the point of naive. Contrary to what their detractors believe, boxing fans do not unconditionally identify with the superior boxer's display of physical violence as he pummels his opponent into senselessness. What the sport of boxing stages in the ring, under admittedly few restraints, is the fighters' confrontation with potential death. Like Roman gladiators, boxers will win the admiration and love of the crowd only if they have been in the dramatic situation of facing personal physical destruction.

No other career in the history of boxing makes this fascination more obvious than the life of Jack Dempsey, one of the great heavyweight champions. As Dempsey himself wrote in the foreword to a biography published in 1929, shortly after his retirement, he "may not have been the best heavyweight of all time," but he dominated his sport during the early 1920s, the golden age of modern boxing. Rather than technique and elegance (which he did have to a certain degree), Dempsey stood for raw physical energy and willpower. He had been born in 1895 as the ninth child of Mormon parents at Manassa, a small coalmining community in Colorado. On his way to the world championship, Dempsey acquired the ring name of the Manassa Mauler, which fused his social origins with his athletic style. In the 1920s and 1930s, he attracted several "sensational" crowds of more than a hundred thousand spectators, and he was the star of the first boxing match that produced a gate of over a million dollars. But while he was a hugely successful draw, Dempsey, for the longest time, was not a popular heavyweight champion. His status was comparable to that of the young Mike Tyson: lots of people wanted to see him fight, but few wanted to see him win.

After allowing Dempsey to take a long hiatus from the ring, his promoters organized a title bout against a young up-and-coming former Marine, Gene Tunney. The fight took place in Philadelphia on September 23, 1926, in an open-air stadium under pouring rain. With 144,468 spectators, it drew the single largest crowd in the history of boxing, and one of the larger crowds in the history of any sport. From the first of ten grueling rounds, Dempsey never stood a remote chance of winning the fight, and the crowd seemed to enjoy this fact. Here is the *New York Times'* description of round one:

> Tunney puts a right glancing blow to Jack's jaw, but it doesn't bother Jack at all. They are in the center of the ring. Jack backs away from Tunney's lead and takes a light right on the face. He backs away to the ropes. Jack does not show the speed he is accustomed to

showing. It is not the Jack we are accustomed to at all . . . Everybody is howling, "Dempsey is groggy!" but he does not look so to me. This is not the Jack Dempsey we are accustomed to see . . . Tunney hit him at least six times with rights and lefts to the face, and Jack gets another on the eye as the bell rings. The first round: Tunney's round by a mile.

Nine rounds later, when Tunney, wrapped in white towels, was declared the undisputed winner by points, the crowd applauded the new champion, but nothing more. Dempsey, by contrast, was "a sorry, pitiful subject. His nose and mouth were spouting blood, his left eye, bruised and battered, was closed tight, and bleeding. There was a cut under his left eye an inch long." But as he left the ring, something uncanny happened. The "strangely silent and unenthusiastic crowd" suddenly started yelling and shouting Dempsey's name. In the course of this life-threatening defeat, Dempsey had been transfigured into a hero.

Years later, in yet another biography, Jack Dempsey drew the right conclusion about this mood swing among the spectators of his 1926 fight: "To my surprise, I was loudly cheered, as I marched from the ring, more than I had ever been cheered before. People were screaming, 'Champ, Champ!' Could it be that the loss was really a victory?" Gene Tunney retired a few years later as unbeaten heavyweight champion of the world, but throughout his flawless career he never became a popular boxer. Joe Louis, by contrast, who lost an early fight in a knockout by the aging German champion Max Schmeling, began his second ascent in the late 1930s, and on his way to the top he gained the adoration of fans. For many boxers, suffering a dramatic defeat seems to be a necessary condition for entering the pantheon of their sport.

But if the main attraction of boxing is to put a fighter in close proximity to death, this does not mean that strategic intelligence, technical prowess, and above all grace of movement are excluded from the attributes that make boxers' bodies shine in the perception of their fans. Natural athletic talent, together with the even more unusual gift of finding the right words to promote his achievements, gave Cassius Clay, a young gold medalist at the 1960 Olympics in Rome, the aura of an eccentric champion. But the fights that "The Greatest of All Times" will always be remembered for, the

fights that produced Muhammad Ali's incomparable status in the history of boxing, were fights in
which he suffered to the verge of physical destruction.

I am thinking of his three matches with Joe
Frazier and, above all, of the aging Ali's epic fight
against the young and physically superior world
champion George Foreman, which took place in
the Zairian capital of Kinshasa on October 30,
1974 (this fight became the central episode in the
film *Ali*). Willingly leaning against the ropes, slid-
ing and moving away as best he could (what Ali
later called his rope-a-dope strategy), and receiving
a brutal beating, mostly against his rib cage, for
seven rounds, Muhammad Ali turned around the
dynamics of the fight in the eighth round when, as
if out of the blue, he hit Foreman decisively with a
left hook, a right to the jaw, and another left hook.
In this match and in his next bout—a narrow victory over Joe Frazier that Ali described as "the clos-
est thing to dying I know of"—it became clear,
once and for all, where the fascination of boxing
lies. It is about suffering to the point of near-death
and then, if possible, returning from the near-
death experience to decisive physical dominance.

Different from bullfighting, which, like boxing,

stages and celebrates a brush with death, boxing does not offer the possibility of a glorious death in the ring itself, in front of fans. The death of a boxer is always an accident, not part of the match. But on those rare occasions when it occurs, sympathy of course flows toward the victim. As Arrachion of Phigalia was competing for his third unlikely win in the merciless Olympic pankration in 564 BC, his much younger opponent suffocated him during the fight. Never more admired than at the moment of his death, Arrhachion was declared the posthumous victor even though he did not win the match.

As the object of spectators' fascination with suffering, boxing is not isolated nor unique, though in some other sports the suffering may be as much mental as physical. All sports that feature a direct confrontation between two opponents—a duel in the most literal sense—stage a scene where composure in the face of gestures of destruction is the highpoint of the production. This is certainly true for wrestling, where avoiding a pin is almost as good as a tie. And it is true for fencing, however reduced the permitted impact of physical violence may be. Less intuitively, the same basic scenario produces the tense excitement of great chess matches, and explains why chess champions need an astonishing level of physical conditioning. As Garry Kasparov, the former world chess champion and one of the great chess players of all times, once explained, without such endurance chess players today could not stay mentally focused during their grueling competitions. Could the stress of this head-to-head confrontation be somehow responsible for the mental illness that afflicts so many great chess champions, foremost among them the elusive American genius Bobby Fischer?

Composure, calm, and resilience during one-on-one combat also describes the requirements of singles tennis. The goal of each serve, each game, set, or match point is to break the opponent's concentration. Like boxers, great tennis players have a game face that unnerves their opposition. Think of the visages of Martina Navratilova and John McEnroe when they threw the ball in the air for the serve and stared at their challengers. And recall how cold the ritual of shaking hands across the net can be at the end of a big tennis match, especially when the winner is, once again, Venus or Serena Williams. All tennis players suffer defeats as well as victories, but those who give in to mental anguish do not make it to the top of their sport. The three-times Wimbledon champion Boris Becker, once his fearless teenage years were over, developed a habit of engaging in self-punishing monologues before decisive points. In the face of potential destruction, he simply became unglued.

In some sports the proximity to death comes from extreme physical exhaustion rather than the physical or mental assault of an opponent. This is the case with long-distance running and alpinism. Bicycle races like the Giro d'Italia or the Tour de France also fascinate spectators in this way. Jan Ullrich has been the second strongest bicycle racer of the Lance Armstrong era and perhaps the most multitalented athlete of his sport. Yet Ullrich did not garner the admiration of fans outside Germany until his punishing defeats in the mountain stages of the Tour de France began to carve lasting traces on his body. Medical research has made it clear that bicycle racing entails a higher level of physical exhaustion than any other sport. But most of the time the opponent whose threatened closeness motivates this self-destructive effort is quite literally out of sight.

Grace

IF THE WORD GRACE had only the superficial meaning that comes to mind in everyday use (which is seldom enough today), I would probably not have chosen it to describe Muhammad Ali's boxing style. But *grace* or *graceful* can be more than just decorative words to note the charm of a teenager or the sway of a ballet dancer. Grace belongs to those concepts which, when examined and thought through, reveal surprising insights and unexpected complexity. In his essay "Ueber das Marionettentheater" ("On String Puppet Theater"), written in 1810, Heinrich von Kleist, one of the greatest authors in the German literary tradition, developed an understanding of grace (the German word he uses is *Anmut*) that helps us appreciate the fascination this quality holds for every true sports fan.

Kleist's fictional dialogue opens with a famous ballet dancer confessing how much he has always enjoyed watching marionettes and how he sees in their movements a model for his own performance. This statement, with its implicit admiration of a popular form of entertainment, must have been much more provocative in Kleist's world than it would be today. But the main thrust of Kleist's provocation, in a time when the highest goal of literature and art was to express the most intimate musings of an individual's soul, lies in the counterintuitive reasons the dancer gives for his fascination with puppets. Instead of emphasizing the shapes and movements marionettes share with the human body, the dancer praises them for belonging to "the realm of the mechanical arts." Grace, Kleist makes us understand, is a function of how distant a body and its movements appear to be from consciousness, subjectivity, and their expression. The gracefulness of puppets lies in their inability to become self-reflexive and thus either embarrassed by or proud of themselves. Grace turns upside down all the accepted knowledge about the relation between the human body and the human mind. It allows the marionettes, as Kleist's ballet dancer so enthusiastically relates, to have their "soul in the elbow" and to touch the ground with a lightness that escapes the laws of gravity. Grace, as an object of aesthetic experience, reminds us how we are sometimes unable—happily unable, I should add—to associate the body movements we see with the intentions or thoughts of those who carry them out.

This complex, dehumanizing impression is what made the performances of Jesse Owens and Wilma Rudolph, the two greatest short distance runners of the twentieth century, so incomparably beautiful. Their bodies and legs, instead of following instructions from the brain, seemed as though they were commanded by some higher force—or perhaps by some mathematical formula. Although Rudolph's legs were uncannily long, there was never a moment when her movements appeared grotesque or unnatural. Different from her competitors in the 1960 Olympics, who were concentrated on the goal line of the 100-meter, 200-meter, and 400-meter relay events, Rudolph appeared to be surprised whenever the goal line came near, as if it was difficult, unpleasant almost, to slow down the rhythm of her stride. In the 1936 Olympics, Owens, despite his charming smile, appears almost apologetic for breaking the world record in the long jump without having an appropriate technique—he seems embarrassed for simply being so superior.

Most track and field events, through their structure and rules, are designed to produce and reward grace, both in practice and, with greater intensity, in moments of competition. Think of the discus, javelin, hammer, or shot-put events—or all the different foot races, from the 100 meters to the marathon. Among winter sports, consider speed skaters' rhythmic glide over the ice, as though in slow motion (such a special treat that I hope, just once, to watch an entire speed skating event live), or imagine the high-speed softness in the movements of downhill skiers as they make their life-risking descents. The challenge, in each case, is to push farther, faster, higher in a specific sequence of body movements (running, jumping, throwing) that are performed under and shaped by detailed constraints. By performing these movements endless times, athletes program their bodies, so that knowledge moves from their brains to the nerves and muscles in their arms and legs ("the soul in the elbow")—and thanks to recent research in cognitive science, this is becoming an empirical description rather than just a metaphor. Athletes' performance may indeed improve in proportion to the distance they gain from consciousness and from the realm of intentions.

Perhaps the lack of direct, face-to-face competition in many track and field events explains why, with very few exceptions, these competitions never draw large crowds, and why those spectators who do watch with passion are mostly themselves practicing athletes. For this select group of fans, the grace that their heroes display may represent the return of human bodies to a state of nature, redeemed from dependence on the mind and brain for survival. Perhaps swimmers go even further, embodying a fantasy of full immersion in an element of the natural world. And for all the sophisticated equipment required to play golf, a beautiful swing partakes of grace, which more than anything else may account for the addictive fascination of this sport. Finding and losing their ideal swing is not something that golfers can fully control, as the career of the prodigious Tiger Woods makes abundantly clear. Even the progress of a rowboat or the stately glide of a sailboat can show grace in this elementary sense—which only confirms that grace is less exclusively attached to any specific sports event than most other sports fascinations.

Grace and violence often go together. Muhammad Ali's movements would not have lost any of their grace if he had been a more hard-hitting boxer. Teófilo Stevenson, the three-times heavyweight gold medal winner from Cuba at the Olympics in 1927, 1976, and 1980 was the one boxer who could have matched Ali's elegance and was probably superior to him in the power of his punch, though for obvious political reasons they never confronted each other in the ring. Despite the sumolike bodies of famous weightlifters (at least in the upper divisions), I can also find grace in the decisive moments of these contests when concentration, overwhelming muscle power, and almost equally overwhelming kilos of iron build up to a moment of do or die. Being able to bring such elements into a transitory harmony is what makes a true weightlifting champion.

A particularly beautiful sport that fuses grace with violence is the Japanese martial art of kendo. Kendo athletes wear garments (I would never dare call them uniforms) that look archaic to Westerners, and they use a two-handed wooden sword. In a strict sense, kendo is nonviolent because the weapon is not supposed to touch the opponent's weapon, let alone his body, except in highly prescribed ways. It is probably this rule (a rule that allows for endless interpretations based on the Zen Buddhist notion of gaps between things through which energy can emerge) that gives the whipping movements of kendo attacks—the athletes' sudden advances and withdrawals—a truly captivating swiftness, as light and energetic as a spring. Heinrich von Kleist, had he known about kendo, probably would have approved.

Tools

SINCE GREEK AND ROMAN antiquity, competitions involving horses have caught the attention of very large crowds. While no genealogical line leads from the chariot races at Olympia and the Circus Maximus to today's NASCAR and Formula One, it is plausible to think that such events were functionally equivalent in their respective historical contexts—a challenge, perhaps, to our notion of discontinuity in the history of sports. Equestrian competitions also call into question another assumption we have made about sports: that sports emerge from specific movements of the human body only. Car racing, one of the most popular and financially successful spectator sports today, poses the same problem of definition. Different from simulations on computer games, these events require a pronounced involvement of the human body with an accessory or tool, but the body's relation to a car or horse is different from its relation to a discus, baseball glove, or pair of skis. For animals and machines are not just objects whose handling demonstrates the strength and skill of the body that handles them. The fascination of sports involving animals and machines relies on the sense that these nonhuman elements are somehow coupled to the human body. The symbiotic relationship between human and tool is the fourth sports fascination I want to explore.

We can see "tools" like horses and cars as extensions or as complexifications of the human body in a double sense. First, they make it possible to go beyond the limits of an exclusively human performance, by, for example, multiplying the maximum speed at which a body can move through space. The second aspect is more difficult to describe, but it gets at the specific challenge such couplings pose to athletes, and helps explain why some perfor-

mances are superior to others. Rather than emphasizing the ability of tools to enhance human abili-
ties, this second aspect emphasizes the ability of a
human to adapt his body to the form, movements,
or function of the tool. It is about the mechanics of
the interface through which bodies and their tools
become connected. Success depends on an inherent paradox: the more perfectly an athlete manages
to adapt his body to the form and movements of a
horse or car, the better he will control them and
the more he will maximize his body's effectiveness.

It does not take a horseman to know that a
jockey who constantly uses the whip will not, in
the end, win as many races as a jockey who lets his
own body movements be carried and shaped by
the stride of the horse. In the final seconds of a
close race, the body of the jockey, bent flat over the
horse's neck, seems to become longer and longer as
it adapts itself to the horse's rhythm. This is the
dynamic shape in which fans remember great
horses and their riders: Eddie Arcaro and Citation,
for example, or Red Pollard and Seabiscuit (the
strangely prosaic ring of many famous racehorse
names would be an interesting poetic phenomenon to analyze). In dressage events, the union be-

tween horse and rider and the harmony they
jointly achieve is the very core of the performance
itself—it is the thing on which winning or losing is
judged. With six Olympic gold and two bronze
medals, as well as numerous world championships
in the 1970s and 1980s, Dr. Reiner Klimke and his
horse Ahlerich were not only two of the all-time
greats of their sport, but they also earned specific
admiration for their flawless mutual understanding (understanding here being the metaphor for a
harmony that cannot be built on concepts).

"Set-up" is the equivalent term used in those
sports where a human body is coupled to an en-
gine. Depending on the shape of the race track,
the competition, weather conditions, and the pit
crew, drivers invest several days in finetuning their
cars to maximize specific strengths and neutralize
weaknesses under the given circumstances. A track
with many turns demands a different set-up from a
track with long straightaways. Truly eminent drivers like Tazio Nuvolari and Juan Manuel Fangio,
Jochen Rindt and Nicki Lauda, Ayrton Senna and
Michael Schumacher make a decisive difference in
the set-up through their combination of mechanical know-how and body-based intuition. Top driv-

ers must also excel by a number of further performance measures that car racing shares with other sports. They must be capable, for hours, of being lost in focused intensity. They have to stay composed despite the continuous threat of death —a tension that dissolves only when they cross the finish line. And finally, they must have phenomenal physical endurance. These multiple challenges probably account for the huge crowds that Formula One and NASCAR events attract—although what they offer to the individual spectator, as live events, are only fragments of the ongoing competition. Being in the presence of greatness, for spectators at a car race, means catching the centaurlike silhouette of the driver for a few short seconds as it passes by at full speed several times during an afternoon. This silhouette loses its fascination as soon as it slows down.

It is an interesting question whether the broad range of shooting competitions belong in this category of "tools." Are firearms different from a javelin or a discus? I think they are. Because instead of making obvious an individual body's strength, firearms enable this body to improve on a certain function—the function of hitting a target. But can we also say that firearms are coupled to human bodies, as horses or racecars undoubtedly are? Are they not mere instruments? Those who engage in shooting certainly are much invested in an almost personal relationship with their weapons. They can tell us long stories about how their bodies got used to the forms of particular firearms. The most impressive evidence in support of such stories probably comes from biathlon athletes who, after long kilometers of a stressful cross-country race on skis, have to find a calm breathing rhythm before they initiate their shooting exercises.

More visibly than most other sports, these hybrid performances of humans and their animals or machines have their origins in the everyday world. And while this makes it easy for some car owners to feel like colleagues of Michael Schumacher, the distance between everyday driving and car racing is desirable not only for practical reasons (foreigners often complain about the Formula One driving style on German freeways) but for aesthetic reasons as well. The German proverb "All happiness of earth lies on the back of horses" probably does not reflect any actual experience; but what it evokes is the fantasy of being a perfect rider, the first and only rider, of a perfect horse, in fluid synchrony with the rhythms of nature. The fascination of the racetrack and speedway lies in this melding of extraordinary human bodies to superior animal or mechanical force.

Forms

IN SPORTS LIKE figure skating, skijumping, gymnastics, and diving, the behavior of judges is a much despised sideshow. Far from being respected by most spectators and athletes, judges are barely tolerated as a necessary evil at these events. One practical reason for the low esteem in which they are held is the absence of objective criteria for determining a winner, and the opportunity, therefore, for the incursion of bias. Fans of gymnastics or figure skating quite regularly believe that judges are being scandalously nationalistic or at least biased—or perhaps have even been bribed—when they give low marks to the fans' favorite competitors. This threat of partiality is inherent in the role of the judge, and it is therefore hard to imagine how sensible improvements could be made to the system.

A more interesting reason for discontent with judges is that they interfere with the ability of great athletes to let new and interesting things happen in their sport. Achieving the impossible, letting loose, being in the zone—these phrases capture our desire to see athletic performances that are unencumbered by restrictions and controls. Something happens to bodies in the great moments of sports, something bodies were not made for. Letting these things happen is incompatible with the act of judging, which has as its goal assigning merit (or lack thereof) to an athlete's ability to perfectly fulfill a prescribed form. Is there a way out of this dilemma? Not really, I think, as long as competing and winning are a part of these sports. And without such components, these events would no longer *be* sports.

One can of course hope that judges will develop a greater awareness of the role that taste (as opposed to stable, measurable criteria) plays in the history of sports, and will become more flexible in their judging practice. This has already happened in ski jumping, where a new, more dynamic style has taken over. The ideal shape for an athlete's body to take as he performs his jump has become much more fluid. Figure skating, by contrast, and at least some routines in gymnastics, seems to have suffered from their judges' ambition to maintain an obsolete standard of beauty appropriated from classical ballet. Despite the outmoded taste of at least some judges, what has kept spectators keenly interested in figure skating, ski jumping, diving, and gymnastics is the willingness of truly exceptional athletes to reject these explicitly aesthetic criteria of their sport and take the risk of achieving what no norm has predefined. But before we can say how such exceptional athletes take care of the problem with judges, we have to explain, with greater precision, in what the fascination of their sports lies.

The fascination of figure skating can be described as the challenge of adjusting an individual body, at a specific moment and within a given time limit, to a sequence of predefined complex forms. To impress the judges means above all to fulfill their expectation that certain forms will be precisely executed. By contrast, pushing the limits of the sport means going for ever higher levels in the complexity of the forms involved. This is what the greatest of the great gymnasts, divers, ski jumpers, and skaters have been doing, instead of merely adapting their bodies, with endless perfection, to the stale criteria of judges' taste.

Japanese gymnasts, among them the never-to-be-forgotten Takashi Ono, revolutionized their sport during the 1950s and 1960s with routines whose forms were as surprising and beautiful as they were daring. These gymnasts thus established a respectful distance between themselves and the rather oppressive German tradition of *Turnen,* which emphasized more militaristic values of body symmetry and control within a largely stable canon of forms. But the most incisive change in the history of gymnastics was the appearance at the 1976 Montreal Olympics of fourteen-year-old Nadia Comaneci from Romania. She changed women's gymnastics forever at a moment when the style developed by the Soviet team under the influence of classical Russian ballet seemed to have become the uncontested international norm. Comaneci not only charmed judges and spectators with a grace that perhaps only teenage girls can embody, but her routines were objectively more complex, and she presented them at a higher speed and with more athleticism than any woman gymnast had done before her. By returning her sport to the value of agon (though most likely without thinking much about aesthetic theory or Greek precedents), Nadia Comaneci invented and embodied a new, dazzlingly complex ideal of gymnastic beauty that delighted spectators around the world.

In the next decade, the American Greg Louganis became the agent of a similar change in diving events. At first glance, Louganis seemed to be at a disadvantage: his body was more muscular and certainly heavier than the bodies of his Chinese competitors, which made it more difficult for him to adapt to the prescribed forms of the most challenging dives. But in decisive moments of his career, Louganis took higher risks than other divers, in terms of complexity, innovation, and daring (for which he sometimes paid with defeats and injuries, one of which became famous because it led him to announce publicly that he had tested positive for HIV). Thanks to this ambitious risk-taking, Louganis was sometimes able to perform breathtaking dives that made spectators declare him the winner even before the judges announced their marks. In the 1988 Olympics—where, competing against athletes half his age, he became the first diver to win two gold medals in each of two consecutive Olympics—Louganis's performance was a sublime moment. Like only a few other athletes in the history of modern sports, he gave his fans the certainty that they were in the presence of greatness.

Plays

FOR ALMOST A CENTURY now, ballgames have fascinated larger crowds worldwide than any other type of sports. Their popularity is a truly global phenomenon. Regional preferences vary, of course—rugby competes with soccer in the southern hemisphere; the United States, the Caribbean, Japan, and Korea are the promised lands of baseball; and cricket is followed with passion throughout the countries that formerly belonged to the British Empire—but not a single country is left, to my knowledge, where a ballgame of some kind is not the predominant spectator sport today. Historians have offered plausible explanations for most of the regional preferences, but some variations remain enigmatic and therefore all the more interesting. One of my favorite open questions about sports is why rugby, dominated by teams from South Africa, Australia, and New Zealand, has established itself so firmly in the southern hemisphere.

On the other hand, as our brief survey of the history of sports has suggested, the fascination with ballgames shows historically- as well as geographically-specific features. In the early decades of the twentieth century, for the first time, watching ballgames reached tidal-wave heights of popularity. Perhaps those decades hold an answer to the question why sports in general have become so hugely important in the past 120 years—and perhaps they could help us understand what larger forces move human emotions in the direction of athletic performance today. As tempting as these big questions might be, I prefer to turn my attention back to the experiences and biases of my own baby-boomer generation.

Like so many other people my age, I feel an al-

most irresistible urge to canonize the mid-twentieth century as the finest years in the history of
ballgames. Or to put it more cautiously, although I
take for granted that the strongest teams today
would prevail over the best teams of that great past
in any imaginary contest, probably few fans today
would say that the ballgame they most love is in
its golden age—as, for example, fans of boxing
or long-distance running said in the 1920s. The
golden age of baseball, without any doubt, was
the second quarter of the twentieth century, when
Babe Ruth, Lou Gehrig, and the young Joe Di-
Maggio played for the greatest baseball team of all
time, their New York Yankees. The legacy from
that period, even more than the franchise's annual
record-breaking budget, is the main reason why
the Yankees still enjoy such exceptional status today.

In American football, my candidate for the most
accomplished and most innovative professional
team ever is the San Francisco 49ers of the 1980s,
when Joe Montana, Jerry Rice, and Roger Craig
ruled the turf. For basketball and hockey, the end
of their golden age may be closer to our own time,
marked by the retirement of Michael Jordan and

Wayne Gretzky. More clearly than in other ball-games, the quasi-mythic golden age of soccer was the time between the 1950s and the early 1980s when Edson Arantes do Nascimento, called Pelé, the Brazilian king of world soccer (whom Brazilians call *O Re,* The King, even today) was at his peak. His career overlapped with Mané Garrincha, Alfredo di Stefano, Ferenc Puskas, Gianni Rivera, Sandro Mazzola, as well as with the smooth Eusebio from Lisbon, the impeccable George Best from Manchester, the Dutch rebel Johann Cruyff, the Bavarian "Emperor" Franz Beckenbauer, and the explosive Diego Maradona from Buenos Aires.

Those decades also featured the long unbeaten Hungarian national team, which tragically lost the final of the 1954 World Cup against a rather mediocre German team and never bounced back from this shock and humiliation; the Real Madrid, whose victories made the title of European champion as coveted as the World Cup; and the Brazilian national team, which won its first of five world championships in 1958 against Sweden at Stockholm by a score of 5:2, while showcasing seventeen-year-old Pelé as its rising star. The confession I am about to make may be in bad taste (the truth can be tacky sometimes), but the names of the five offensive players on Brazil's 1958 team still sound like beautiful samba lyrics to me: Garrincha, Didi, Vavá, Pelé, Zagalo. (For those of you who cannot remember this time as though it was yesterday, there once were five exclusively offensive players in soccer.)

So much for nostalgia. Perhaps the reason we have somehow less appreciation for the great individual players and teams of today is simply that there are so many of them. Maybe it is a paradox of sorts: having such an assortment of accomplished athletes makes it difficult for even the best among them to shine as brightly as the great players from an earlier age. But as I am proposing this argument, frankly I do not believe in it. For soccer, despite all the talk about new styles, new strategies, and greater efficiency, the most admired and perhaps even the most successful players continue to be those that remind us of the best athletes during soccer's golden age. The Brazilian national team and dozens of individual Brazilian players in all major leagues of the world have dominated more visibly during the past two decades than any other group of athletes in the history of soccer, although they hardly ever satisfy the rather abstract, pragmatic, and "modern" expectations of coaches and critics in the European professional leagues. The playful and not always very efficient Ronaldinho (who was selected as International Player of the Year in 2004) is a more admirable athlete than Real Madrid's streamlined Brazilian goalgetter, Ronaldo. Zinedine Zidane, perhaps the greatest soccer player of the past decade, is not the fastest athlete on his team, nor does he score as many goals as Ronaldo. But the elegance of his movements and his passes are so delightful.

What we enjoy in the great moments of a ballgame is not just the goal, the touchdown, the home run, or the slamdunk. It is the beautiful individual play that takes form prior to the score. What a form is we intuitively know. The sociologist and philosopher Niklas Luhmann has defined it as the paradoxical union of the difference between self-reference and outside reference. This simply means that a form is any phenomenon with the capacity of presenting itself to our senses and experience in clear distinction from everything that is not a part of it.

But a beautiful play is more than just a form—it

is an epiphany of form. A beautiful play is produced by the sudden, surprising convergence of several athletes' bodies in time and space. Beautiful plays are surprising for two reasons. Even if the specific form is what specialists call a set play—a play designed and rehearsed endless times—it will be new and surprising for the average spectator who is not familiar with the team's playbook. But beyond that, plays that emerge in the real time of a ballgame are surprising even for coaches and the players who perform them, because they must be achieved against the unpredictable resistance of the other team's defense. While the team in possession of the ball tries to create a play and avoid chaos, its opposing team in the defensive position tries to destroy the emerging form and precipitate chaos. (The offense can be said to embody the principle of negentropy, while the defensive line embodies the principle of entropy.)

In addition to being complex, embodied, and surprising, a beautiful play is also a temporalized form. This means that the play begins to vanish from the very moment it begins to emerge. As soon as the quarterback throws the ball in a receiver's direction, intuitively knowing at the moment of release where the receiver will be a second or two later, the play, including all the complex routes that several players have to perform to make the play possible, will begin to disappear. No still photograph can ever capture the beauty of this temporalized reality. And there are few experiences that make my heart beat faster than a beautiful play. Depending on whether my team or the opposing team produces it, I will be profoundly happy or profoundly sad by the time it vanishes. But looking back later, after hours, days, or years, I often realize that a beautiful play produced even by the opposing team has turned into a happy memory.

The rules of different ballgames allow the staging of an overwhelming variety of plays that could be analyzed and described endlessly. I will limit myself to some of the most obvious and elementary principles. Games that allow players to secure the ball with their hands and thus make the plays of the team in possession of the ball more predictable (like basketball, American football, or rugby) have a tendency to develop elaborate repertoires of set plays that coaches carry out in chesslike battles with strategists on the other side. Games like soccer or hockey, by contrast, with their lower degree of ball or puck control, entail less predictability and rely more on the intuition and initiative of individual players. Also, games with a high degree of ball control tend to allow aggressive tackling by the defense, whereas those with less control allow less. Baseball is an extreme case of the latter. It has been said that no movement in any sport is technically more demanding—or more dangerous—than using a bat to hit a small hard ball that comes toward you at a speed close to a hundred miles per hour. This explains why the batter is allowed to concentrate on his hitting without having to worry about interference from defensive players.

Interestingly, this equation between the degree of ball control and the intensity of tackling is turned on its head in some sports. In basketball, for example, despite a high degree of ball control, the defensive players are not allowed to make body contact. This fact, together with the comparatively small surface of the basketball court, leads to the high scores, fast pace, and artistic flavor of the game—and above all to those fascinating instants when players on the court suddenly stop moving, as though in freeze-frame. Hockey, by contrast, allows for defensive plays with full body impact despite the fact that a puck skidding across ice is very difficult to control. These two factors keep scores comparatively low but allow a high level of unpredictability, including frequent turnaround situations and surprising fast breaks.

Are ballgames reaching the limit of human performance today, as has happened in sports like bodybuilding, gymnastics, figure skating, diving, and so many track and field events? For all practical purposes the answer is no, although the hand-eye coordination and batting power in baseball may be exceptions. Fans will always imagine that their heroes could play a little harder, throw a little faster, jump a little higher, and certainly make a larger percentage of free throws than they already do. The real question is, then, whether an ever higher level of physical performance (and perhaps also strategic complexity) could not end up becoming aesthetically counterproductive, at least for some ballgames. If, contrary to the opinions of most coaches and specialists, I am right in saying that scoring and winning are not what exclusively fascinates fans, could it be that some ballgames, during the past decades, have crossed a dangerous line of optimization, where efficiency begins to turn against aesthetic enjoyment?

Although no African team has ever come close to winning the soccer World Cup, many fans like myself wish that old-fashioned-looking African soccer would establish itself as the soccer of the future. A similar nostalgia applies to professional football and baseball in the United States. In their striving for strategic advantage and athletic preparation, these popular sports may be losing some of the fascination that has held generations of fans in thrall. Not for random reasons, the National Hockey League has been struggling with offside rules that maximize defensive efficiency at the expense of offensive performance, which above all produces beauty on the ice. Perhaps this aging fan's nostalgia for what he calls the golden age of team sports will turn out to have some grounding in empirical facts.

I have said a lot about beautiful plays. But what would an ugly play in sports look like? When would we say that a play is not beautiful? These questions were asked by my friend Toshi Hayashi toward the end of a discussion at Kyoto—one of the few major cities in the world without any dominant team sport franchise. One easy answer is obvious: what we often call ugly are cases of foul play. But this, strictly speaking, is not really an answer, because foul plays interrupt the game and are therefore not a part of it. The more important observation facilitated by Hayashi's question is that the aesthetics of sports do not seem to provide negative concepts. We may call some exaggerated effects of bodybuilding ugly, and we may use this word for a jump in a skating competition or for a movement in gymnastics that grotesquely fails to fulfill the form it was supposed to become. But even in such a case, it would be rather unusual to used the word "ugly." In general, and for the more popular sports, we only feel a lack—a lack of exciting plays in ballgames, a lack of drama in boxing, a lack of grace in track and field. Once a play emerges in a ballgame, we are captured by what we see. But when such moments do not arrive, we do not call this lack ugly.

Timing

EVERYONE KNOWS THAT time matters in many different athletic events. Lots of records are registered and expressed in temporal measures, and many critical moments in team sports are intensified by how much time is left on various clocks. For example, the supplementary time in soccer called injury time has recently acquired a Homeric aura, at least for decisive games, because during the scarce minutes of injury time decisive goals are more likely to happen. But clock-watching does not seem to be the right approach for a discussion of time as a source of fascination in sports, because it keeps us in a purely quantitative dimension. A more promising topic is the phenomenon of timing—the capacity to make the right movements at the right time.

Timing is probably best explained by calling on athletes' own experience. Athletes know that, at decisive moments in a competition, the flux of time seems to be suspended—or at least enormously dilated. This is the meaning of the (interestingly enough) spatial metaphor of "being in the zone" that some athletes use for a specific time-related dimension of experience. Here is how an outstanding college football player described it:

> When a player has entered the zone, a state of hypersensitivity and tension has taken place.

This explains the apparent ease during my run toward the end zone. It is not that I am not working as hard as the other players on the field. It is just that in this state of hyper-sensitivity, things are moving so much slower than they are for the rest of the players on the field. My senses are much more aware of what is going on around me and that enables all of the triggers inside of me to react a little faster than the other players, making me appear more fluent.

Although Stanford running back J. R. Lemon, to whom I owe this beautiful paragraph, does not avoid time-related descriptors, he clearly speaks about a decisive transformation of what we normally refer to when we talk about time in sports. He concentrates on a spatial metaphor ("the zone") in order to evoke the condition of his good timing. As soon as he is in the zone, he no longer perceives how fast he is running. He does not feel pressed. Movements that seemed to be difficult to achieve before he was in the zone now become easy, quiet, and natural. Paradoxically, it is the receding of time pressure that allows for good timing—for finding the right moment that corresponds to each body movement in a given spatial context.

Once he is in the zone and sees the game as if in slow motion, a running back like Lemon will spot the gaps in the opposing team's defensive line and will believe that he has (and will indeed have) enough time to make his way through those gaps while they are still open. This description also applies to the timing of great tennis players, who take advantage of any extraneous movement performed by their opponents. Or to long-distance runners, who find the moment for an intermediary sprint when competitors are not prepared for the change of pace. Good timing—a temporal phenomenon central to all sports, not just those regulated by clock time—refers to cases of perfect fusion between a perception of space and the initiation of movement. Timing is the intuitive capacity to bring one's body to a specific place at the very moment when it matters to be there. It is a skill, by the way, which up to a certain level can be acquired through practice.

If good timing is crucial to spectators' enjoyment of sports, then this implies that, in many cases at least, violence—or, more precisely, the po-

tential for violence—becomes a central component in our aesthetic appreciation of sports. Violence is the act of occupying spaces or blocking
their occupation by others through the resistance
of one's body. Timing and violence are inseparably
related because timing, at least in ballgames, pre-
supposes that a specific place on the field is the one
and only right place for an individual athlete to be,
with his body, at a certain moment. Depending on
the specific rules of his game, the player will be in
the right place for one of two possible reasons: either because the spot in question will not be occu-
pied (not covered) by the body of another player at
that moment, or precisely because the body of another player *will* occupy it.

Timing, then, is always either about avoiding or
producing violence. In contact sports like hockey,
rugby, and American football (and, behind the referee's back, in soccer and basketball as well), an
athlete wants to be at a certain place at a certain
moment because this means he can target an opposing player's body. In the best case, this produces
the one form of violence that spectators of some of
the sports in question appreciate as a clean hit. In a
clean hit, the body of an athlete has an impact on

the body of another in the right spot, at the right moment, with an immediate effect. The goal of his opponent, by contrast, may be to get open, to occupy a strategically important place that should be but is not covered by a player from the other team.

Making a clean hit and getting open are convex and concave versions, so to speak, of the same form. Both are the product of timing, and they will be perceived as forms even in the most action-packed environment. Seen from the angle of timing, the beauty of a clean hit is difficult to deny—even among those who, for some moral reason, do not like this use of the concept of beauty. But then again, I have never claimed that enjoying sports—or enjoying beauty in general—has much of anything to do with moral improvement.

Looking back to the seven fascinations in this typology of sports and to the preceding historical outline, one can easily imagine an entire book dedicated to the historical distribution of these fascinations (and others) as a complex chapter of cultural history. Here is not the place for such an elaborate exploration, but I do want to highlight some of the more striking observations in question. Given the discontinuity we have seen in the history of sports, it is remarkable that one genre of athletic events seems to have held a continuous fascination throughout the millennia. These are sports that fuse the human body to an animal or machine and thus increase the possibilities of the body's performance. Second, we found at least two striking cases where a fascination returned after thousands of years. Bodybuilding has probably never been more popular than it is today, except for the centuries of Greek antiquity. This return is all the more interesting as it includes a similarity in the forms and implications of behavior that surround the athletic site. Another fascination making a return engagement in our time is composure in the presence of death. It was constitutive for Roman gladiator contests and became popular again with boxing and all kinds of endurance sports during the 1920s. But the greatest intellectual challenge is to understand the comparatively recent emergence of ballgames as the central sports fascination of our time—a fascination so existentially important for many of us that we have a hard time indeed imagining our world without it.

four

GRATITUDE

You HAVE SEEN SUCH pictures in the daily newspapers, and if sports matter to you at all, then you have seen them with intensely mixed emotions. These pictures show a famous former athlete in his mid-thirties, still looking trim and focused as though he is about to make a great catch or hit a decisive home run. But those talented hands are now idle, as the athlete stands in a courtroom receiving his sentence. One part of your reaction is anger and disbelief. How could this hero have wasted his reputation and his future on drug addiction? How could he have become an abusive husband or a negligent father when life had treated him so exuberantly well, gracing him with a unique athletic talent, a charming smile, and the admiration of countless fans? How could a

man who signed several multimillion-dollar con-
tracts during his decade-long professional career
have come to this? The fallen hero's face looks
alert, but you suspect he does not understand what
has happened to him any better than you do. You
have the impression that his mind is not really in
that courtroom, where his once-glorious life has
sunk so low. Is he remembering that autumn
evening when he almost single-handedly won the
World Series for his team? When he was the nation's darling, when TV announcers would have
paid a fortune for a two-minute interview, when
his parents, wife, and children were so proud to be
his family? These are the milder questions evoked
by that merciless newspaper photo.

In other, deeper colors you remember that unforgettable moment when the now-defendant, in
an incomparably intense and energetic movement
of his entire body, hit a curveball that the opposing
pitcher had thrown at him with admirable skill
and the most aggressive intention. As the baseball
rises higher and higher in your memory, flying
over the outfielder's glove and leaving the stadium
behind right field, you begin to realize, with dis-
turbing moral ambivalence, that you cannot really

feel contempt for the damage he has done to himself and to those who have loved him, including his fans. What you so strongly desire is the opposite of justice: if only you could, you would pay a fortune yourself, to buy him one more chance. All you can see in that stark photograph of an uncommon criminal is the former slugger to whom you feel so attached.

This is an emotional dilemma that only a sports fan can experience. You are the watcher, and sometimes life forces you to see not just the wonder but the waste.

Watching

BEING LOST IN focused intensity—the formula cast by the gold-medalist swimmer Pablo Morales—precedes, accompanies, and follows the events of athletic performance. It is their precondition, their actuality, and their yield. It describes both athletes and spectators, and thus helps us to understand a basic (and often overlooked) convergence that occurs despite the different types of body investment on the athletes' and the spectators' side. As soon as we try to distinguish more specific modalities of experience for spectators and athletes, however, a basic asymmetry appears. As for athletes, different sports give different forms to the experience of being lost in focused intensity. And while we could identify, in a similar way, various forms of watching and participating that sports impose upon spectators, I want to highlight just two elementary modes of spectatorship that can be found in all sports, with stronger or weaker individual affinities, of course. I call them *analysis* and *communion*.

Imagine a professional hockey game. All the players except for the goalkeepers rotate on and off the ice in shifts that rarely last longer than two or three minutes. As long as the penalty box is empty, twelve athletes are on the ice at any given moment, and about a dozen players on each team are sitting on the bench, watching the game unfold. The players who are watching try to gather as much insight as possible about the strategy, strengths, and weaknesses of the opposing team. Their mode of spectatorship during this time is predominantly analytic, and as they always return to the ice for another shift, the boundary between these analytic spectators and the players chasing the puck is permeable.

Now turn your attention to the crowd that watches the same hockey game. We tend to think of these spectators as boisterous, emotional, sometimes rapturous as they follow the unfolding events. Above all, though, we think of the crowd as having very little, if any, analytic focus. The thing that fans seem to enjoy most at the hockey rink is being in communion with other enthusiastic fans like themselves. They are not analytical in the way that a player about to take his shift on the ice is analytical, and the boundary between players and these fans is not permeable, at least not at first glance. The fences that used to surround many soccer fields in Europe and the United Kingdom can be thought of as a materialization of this difference. As a crowd spectator myself, I confess there is not a single sport, however modest its physical requirements may be, in which I could actively participate by any stretch of the imagination. Like so many other spectators in the crowd, I sit at a physical, and a categorical, distance from those who compete.

The behavior of spectators like myself is similar then, in some ways, to the investment of a person who bets on a horse or the next day's weather or a football game. The gambler has something at stake, but he has no influence on the outcome of the event in question, and all he can do is hope that the outcome will reward and multiply his investment. While a crowd may not have a financial stake in the outcome of a sports event, these spectators have invested their emotions. They have risked disappointment, perhaps even depression, in exchange for a chance to be present at a dramatic performance. While those who invest money in the "futures" market are often not interested in following the details of price fluctuations—they just want to know, at the end of the day, whether they won or lost their bet—the emotional investment of spectators at a sports event glues them to their seats in the stadium or to their chairs in front of the TV set because every second of action contains a potential payoff in intensity.

Sports spectators in a crowd hope their favorite team will win, but they do not consider their emotional investment or time entirely wasted as long as the game contains excitement. What disappoints fans more than losing is boredom—the lack of action and effort. Nothing is worse than watching a game that neither team really wants to win. Some midseason all-star games, where players concentrate on avoiding situations that might cause an injury, can be deadly boring to watch (and probably to play).

Regardless of whether we consider Spanish bullfights to be a sport or not (and multiple arguments can be made for both positions), they impressively illustrate that crowd emotions may well exist independently of winning or losing. There is no uncertainty about how the bullfight will end. The animal will be killed. The quality of the event thus hinges solely on the violent beauty of the drama that the bull and toreador jointly perform, and it is measured by the emotion, by the *alegría,* that it produces in the crowd. During the best moments of a bullfight, a band playing a *paso doble* will resonate with the intense and fluid emotion of spectators—as if to synchronize aristocratic sensibilities with the primal intensity of ritual killing. Nothing could be further from the collective anxiety about winning or losing a hockey game than this multilayered spectator fascination.

Any type of sport can produce both kinds of spectators—those with an analytical gaze and those with an emotional investment. But each individual sport has a more or less intense affinity with one or the other mode of spectatorship. For example, under normal conditions, few people among the spectators of a swimming event (except perhaps family members of the competitors) have not been active swimmers or swimming coaches themselves at some point in their lives. These spectators watch the races with an analytic eye. And while not every admirer of Formula One events and their fancy cars is a former race car driver, most of them are men (and some women) who pride themselves on their own sporty driving. By contrast, it is difficult—indeed depressing—to imagine a college basketball game where only former players or coaches sit in the stands.

Different styles of communion have developed among fans of different sports in different cultural contexts. The only spectators who look even more relaxed than those watching a test match of cricket, say between the West Indies and Pakistan, are those happy American families who sit on the lawn for several days watching Little League baseball playoffs, dividing their attention between the game and the quality of the hot dogs at the concession stand. At San Francisco Giants games, my wife seems always to have the tough luck of buying drinks and food when the decisive plays are happening, yet she still remains a faithful fan. In Japan, by contrast, baseball fans are as intense and loud as American college football crowds (rumor has it that the Japanese copied their behavior from this sport) or as supporters of F. C. Liverpool in the English Premier Soccer League who, in one mighty voice, sing "You'll Never Walk Alone" to cheer up their heroes. And while the fans of the opposing baseball team may tease you congenially if your seat happens to be in the wrong section of a park, it is dangerous to stand among Liverpool soccer fans if you are rooting for Manchester United. Those who can afford to buy tickets for a boxing gala at a top hotel in Las Vegas are required to wear a tuxedo and a bow tie. But there are other boxing events (and I have been to more than one) where I would have felt grotesquely overdressed in a sports coat. Yet despite all these colorful varieties of spectator sociability, the basic alternative between following the events with an analytic mind or with a high level of emotional investment remains valid.

Although philosophers and poets have hardly ever paid attention to sports spectators, they have accumulated, over the decades, a rich repertoire of concepts that apply to the two sides of this distinction among spectators. The playwright Bertolt Brecht's ideal of a distant spectator comes to mind, a spectator who would smoke (and occasionally even exchange impressions with other spectators) while following, analyzing, and ultimately drawing political insights from watching a play of "epic theater." You will only grasp the imagined merit of this description if you understand it against the backdrop of its opposite, the (for Brecht) undesirable spectator type whom he associates with catharsis and other perhaps ill-understood notions from Aristotle's *Poetics*. For Brecht, this other, Aristotelian spectator embodies what he considered to be the capital sin against intellectual alertness, that is, the desire to identify with heroes on the stage.

Much more famous and much richer indeed is Friedrich Nietzsche's distinction between the Apollonian and the Dionysian attitude. The Apollonian spectator is a type who, from a distance, perceives and appreciates the beauty of individual forms. He is not necessarily analytic in the sense of Brecht's ideal spectator or of hockey players watch-

ing their teammates from the bench, but clearly
the Apollonian spectator has a greater affinity with
the concept of analysis than with the concept of
communion. Dionysian spectators, by contrast,
have a tendency to abandon individuality and
distance altogether and to revel in communion
both with other spectators and with the energy
that emerges from the action they are following.
Among the classical Greek playwrights, Nietzsche
deftly downgraded Euripides because he felt that
Euripides' tragedies did not help the audience
reach this state of Dionysian communion. Rapture
and intoxication were the words with which Nietzsche characterized his own vision of Dionysian
crowds, and he imagined that the intensity of this
participation would in the end lead naturally to a
sleep of profound happiness.

If we were to deal with these polar distinctions
in terms of better or worse, adequate or inade-
quate, more or less intense, we would be trapped
in the "critical" perspective on sports that I want to
avoid. And in fact, different modes of following
sports are so different from one another that they
cannot be compared even qualitatively. For example, the intensity that results from watching tennis

with an analytic eye is quite different from the shiver that comes over fans when their football team is about to win a national championship, but neither is a higher (or lower) mode of spectatorship. Comparing my own distinction between analysis and communion with Nietzsche's two types, I can see that my concepts, rather than describing two exclusive forms of participation, mark two poles of a broad spectrum of possible spectator attitudes. In the middle of this spectrum I imagine a detached enjoyment of movements and forms that is less sharp than analysis and more removed from performing athletes than the crowds desirous of communion.

In recent decades, the Dionysian style has turned out to be more fascinating to philosophers and humanists from other academic disciplines than the Apollonian—perhaps because this mode of spectatorship has a reputation of being unruly. Dionysian rapture is certainly not the attitude toward the world that our parents and teachers recommended to us. With the nightmare of Fascism still haunting the West, our mentors expected us to become rational, analytical *individuals*—a formula for social approval and professional success in every thinkable context. Being part of a crowd, by contrast, and losing control over our emotions and behavior are what we have been warned against since childhood. Consequently, many of us have forgotten (or have never known) what a joy it can be to be part of a crowd. We feel, rather, morally obliged to associate the frenzy of crowds exclusively with those hooligans who make international soccer events physically dangerous places to be.

But for thousands of fans in times past, being part of the crowd at a sports event provided opportunities to immerse themselves in the realm of presence. Imagine the Roman gladiator games and chariot races taking place in the Colosseum or Circus Maximus in the first century AD; imagine the rowdy spectators of *calcio* battles in Renaissance Tuscany; imagine the eighteenth-century boxing contests in London which, in a cultural environment that was otherwise not given to athletic fascination, managed to assemble many thousands of spectators. Those crowds preceded the masses of fans who, after the turn of the twentieth century, started to fill monumental stadiums to watch team sports—crowds that still continue to grow today.

Key in the phenomenology of such crowds at athletic events is the roar that tens of thousands of spectators can jointly produce. It not only inspires their favorite teams; it is a physical point of self-reference through which the crowd perceives and transforms itself into one unified body. In recent decades crowds have also shown a tendency to make themselves not just audible but visible as unified bodies—from wearing the colors of their team and painting their faces to participating in "the Wave" that sometimes sweeps spontaneously around the stadium. There is a typical (and for me favorite) moment in college football when, before a decisive play, team members on the sidelines turn to the crowd and wave their arms to elicit the fans' vocal support. The standard, rational explanation for this gesture is that the noise of the crowd makes verbal communication among the players of the opposing team impossible. However, I believe that something more primal is also at work. As long as crowd noise only makes difficult any verbal communication on the other team, it functions within an interactive dimension. But what many players and fans enjoy about cheering is a state of mind that absorbs and transforms individuality into communion, where the interaction of communication is no longer necessary.

Crowds long for the moment when their combined physical energy connects with the players' energy and makes the players' energy grow. For at that moment, the separation between the crowd and the players seems to vanish. Such a communion, far from being purely spiritual, might constitute a physical reality. It may even have a very real biological basis in the recently discovered mirror neurons in the pre-motor cortex of the brain. Mirror neurons become activated not just when a person performs an action himself but also when he sees someone else perform it. These neurons, or others like them, may turn out to provide a physiological basis for empathy—the emotional link that makes another person's experience seem like our own.

Whatever crowd behavior may exactly be, physical or cultural, the emergence of its energy in and around our individual bodies and in the crowd as a whole is largely independent of winning or losing. Without a doubt, crowds want their energy to help carry their teams to victory. But the same true fans will stay in the stadium, connected emotionally with their team, until the bitter end of a smashing defeat—or even after. When in 1950 Brazil lost the final game of the soccer World Cup, played at home against a team from the tiny neighbor republic of Uruguay, more than fifty thousand of the two hundred thousand spectators who had attended the game stayed in Rio's Maracana stadium, mourning through the entire night. Collecting jerseys, sweatbands, or gloves that players have worn during a game is but one of many rituals that have grown out of a desire for physical oneness.

During the first decades of the twentieth century, many of the then newly constructed stadiums were also used for political party rallies and other carefully choreographed mass spectacles. But we have both documentary evidence and philosophical reason to doubt that the participants of such mass spectacles experienced the frenzy that athletic events regularly produce. I am not speaking of crowds that spontaneously gather in moments of political tension and often explode with uncontrollable energy and violence—the most famous event of this kind being the Prise de la Bastille of July 14, 1789. I refer rather to political rallies or parades on commemorative days such as May 1 or July 4, where the energy level is typically low, probably because everyone shares the same ideology. There is no primordial gap to bridge in these political choreographies, no dissent or division of opinion that could energize the crowd. These party rallies are mostly docile affairs, whereas the event-induced behavior of soccer crowds often turns unpredictable, violent, and dangerous.

Since the 1998 soccer World Cup in France, we know, from evidence confirmed by research, that the traditional psychosociological explanations for the aggression of fans do not hold true. The so-called hooligans who wreak havoc, threatening both their own lives and those of people they hit in their frenzy, are not, for the most part, repressed proletarians who are venting their frustration. Nor are they necessarily even supporters of the losing team. They are collective bodies in rapture, unified and intoxicated by a communal experience that reels out of control. To a large extent, those who make up these out-of-control crowds belong to the wealthier and better-educated social strata. And I have to say, I know the feeling. Happy over a victory or depressed about a defeat, I never feel com-

pletely sober when I leave Stanford Stadium after a
football game, never mind that no alcoholic bever-
ages have been consumed. I may not always wish
to do so, but I know that I need to cool off before
driving my car. This is why I make sure to park ten
or fifteen minutes' walk away from the stadium
gates.

Then again, is this notion of communion not an
outdated and hopelessly romantic description of
sports spectatorship? The contemporary reality is
that most sports fans watch their favorite teams on
television with a few friends or family members,
not in a stadium with a crowd. Even in Brazil, of
all places, the verb for being physically present
at an athletic event, *assistir,* has become the verb
that also refers to watching sports on the screen.
Shouldn't my description of spectatorship as analysis or communion be replaced with a revised notion in which these two modes merge within a
more complex "media system" of spectatorship? I
can certainly anticipate this objection coming
from the direction of media studies (yesterday's academic sensation), and I will immediately concede
that media specialists make a number of important
points. It is true that the economic viability of pro-

fessional sports today depends largely on broadcasting, not on the gate. It is also true that contemporary media technology and the viewing habits
that are emerging under its influence have produced new ways to enjoy sports in real time. And
finally, it is true that those DVDs featuring endless
"highlights" have become so popular that they are
having an impact on the playing style of different
team sports.

But however naive or banal this will sound, I believe that what is decisive for ESPN's Nielsen rat-
ings is still the quality of the games played in the
stadium. Even a DVD collection of the most
amazing slamdunks of all time would not be appealing if those who watch it could not supplement, in their imagination, those multiple
slamdunks with pictures and narratives from actual basketball games. Of course some sports lend
themselves more to fragmentation than others
(basketball more than soccer, figure skating even
more than basketball), but I believe that separating
the beautiful play or the perfectly executed axel
from the larger context of a competitive event
must have an effect of disenchantment.

A more realistic question about the relation between sports and modern media technology is how the latter has changed spectators' viewing habits—and the answer to this question is not surprising at all. Inevitably, the experience of radio listeners and television viewers has shifted toward the more analytic end of the spectrum. Announcers' commentaries are the main reason for this shift, as they cover and interpret the game using a grid of concepts. This grid provides a layer of meaning that puts listeners and viewers at a distance (or rather, perhaps, at a half-distance) from the players' presence. Stadium crowds, by contrast, may be loud or silent but in principle they are not permeated by acts of communication—although in state-of-the-art stadiums, huge screens bring the crowd's experience closer to the mode of a broadcast. Even more than the TV announcers' commentary, electronic tools like replay and slow motion produce an impression of analysis. A broadcast or a replay screen in the stadium can give fans the illusion that they have the same information the coach is using to analyze a play that just happened and to revise his game strategy.

But what broadcasting abandons and cannot replace is the physical co-presence of spectators and athletes as the most elementary condition for communion. Not unlike coaches in their analytic concentration, spectators in front of a television screen are mostly alone while they watch the game—even if they sit together with their families or friends and partly succeed in recreating a stadiumlike atmosphere in their living room. With the exception of unique moments—above all, when their favorite team wins a world championship or when their favorite athlete breaks a world record—spectators in front of a TV set will not grow together into a small crowd. As long as their reality is the TV screen, the plays on the field do not approach their bodies or withdraw from them, and this is bound to change, quite fundamentally, the dynamic of the energy exchange.

But perhaps I should not let myself get so carried away by my preference for the stadium space. Watching sports on television and watching sports in the stadium are simply two different and of course equally legitimate forms of leisure. So different are they that professional franchises and media managers have stopped worrying that broadcasting athletic events will reduce the number of spectators in the stadium. On the contrary, watching sports at home with a more analytic attitude can catch the interest of viewers who have no primary sports fascination, and it is certainly true that they will see more and understand the game better in a TV broadcast. Going to the stadium from time to time may, in turn, enhance the wish to follow a team or a sport on the screen with greater regularity.

My own enthusiasm for stadiums and indoor arenas is so great that it extends to those buildings even during the days and hours when they are empty. However embarrassing this may be to admit, my heart would always beat faster when, twice a day, I drove by the large and endearingly decadent structure of the old Stanford Stadium. Somehow, I had come to love its strange shape— stranded between an ideal stadion from ancient Greece and an arenalike enclosure that never became quite closed enough to make spectators feel like a compact crowd. When I travel to Madrid and walk down La Castellana, the city's most elegant avenue, I feel happy in anticipation of spotting the monumental Estadio Santiago Bernabeu where the proud teams of Real Madrid have dominated the international soccer scene for most of the past half century. I remember my excitement, more than thirty years ago, at first glimpsing the enigmatically asymmetrical shape of Chelsea London's very old stadium, Hammersmith Bridge, where I saw Peter Osgood, then Chelsea's much admired center forward, score a goal from forty yards with amazing precision and where today a Russian billionaire is running an experiment designed to confirm that an unlimited budget can produce athletic greatness. I am depressed each time I read in my morning newspaper about the project to abandon "the house that Ruth built" in the Bronx, in favor of a more modern Yankee Stadium (though it will not be called that if naming rights are sold). And I was therefore delighted to learn that the Boston Red Sox had decided not to abandon Fenway Park, although the strange wall that fans call the Green Monster will forever keep the number of available seats problematically low. But even the enthusiasm of diehard Fenway crowds cannot compete with the fans who gather at Koshien Stadium, Asia's oldest athletic site, built in 1924 half way between Osaka and Kobe. The fans of the Hanshin Tigers, a team whose stats until very recently had been far more depressing than the Red Sox' pre-2004 record, celebrate ecstatic nine-inning love feasts that dilute and absorb, game after game, the frustrating memories of the Tigers' most recent defeat. All by myself, I spent a delightful late afternoon sitting at the open end of the mother of all stadiums in Olympia, at the very spot where Greek athletes started and returned on their races two and a half thousand years ago. And in the harbor district of Buenos Aires, I bribed a janitor at La Bombonera, the stadium of Boca Juniors, to let me sit for a quiet lonesome hour in those famously steep stands. Above all, however, I would like to return to Maracana every year, to the sanctuary of Brazilian soccer, now almost in ruins, to the place where Pelé, The King, produced his magic, as if to exorcise the memory of Brazil's defeat in the 1950 World Cup final.

But how can empty stadiums attract me so much, if they are nothing without an athletic event to move the emotions of the crowd? Let me pose another paradoxical question that will bring us closer to an answer. From a purely economic point of view, why would some of the most expensive real estate in a city be devoted exclusively to events that take place, at most, twice a week, that last for just a few hours, and follow seasonal schedules? Even if, in a (for me) deplorable trend, these stadiums are occasionally filled with the fans of Bruce Springsteen or the followers of Reverend Moon, this revenue does not decisively improve their balance sheet. Since teams do not even conduct their practice sessions in these facilities, wouldn't owners be wise to replace these buildings with high-rises that would produce a much greater yield, and build new modern stadiums at the urban periphery, where air and traffic conditions are so much better? This was the conclusion many franchises drew a few decades ago, but today they are eager to return to the center of big cities. So the question is this: what is it about empty stadiums that not only fascinates me but makes franchise owners and municipal governments willing to maintain these mostly empty structures at such enormous cost?

Far-fetched as this may sound at first, I suspect that stadiums "stage" or "make present" what Martin Heidegger once identified as the most elementary philosophical question: why there is something at all, as opposed to nothing. On many levels and in multiple settings, stadiums materialize, and make us part of, this ultimate ontological contrast.

During the week, while they are closed and quiet, big stadiums are the one place in a bustling city where nothing happens. But on game day, we pour into the stadium, filling the seats and buzzing with our own excitement, and focus our collective attention on the still-empty field. Then, just before gametime, for a unique and thrilling moment, the athletes appear and "take the field." With our hearts beating faster, we rise to join other spectators in a roaring welcome for our heroes. This special moment becomes thickened with complex opening rituals—none perhaps more exuberantly textured than those of American college football.

Or imagine the anxious last-second twitches preceding a horse race, or the statuesque tableau just before a referee drops the puck for an opening faceoff; or the moment when a figure skater, already in her pose, waits for the music to begin. What has been said of music, that the silences are as important as the sounds, also works for stillness and movement in an athletic performance. No sport has taken this tension to a higher level than American football, with its twenty-five seconds before every individual play when two times eleven athletes line up face to face and hold their position as if in freeze-frame. By containing the action for these interminable seconds, the game presents in stark relief the violent clash of bodies and the complex plays that are over almost as quickly as they can be perceived. The tiniest movement by a player on the offensive or defensive line can transform these developing forms back into nothingness, if the referee calls the movement offside. As fans, we become participants in this primordial tension between something and nothing—although we are usually far from understanding the part that we play. Such instants inject us with an energy and a jubilant sense of pleasure that may well become addictive.

Waste

IF YOU HAPPEN TO agree with me, based on your own experience as a spectator (or, if you are not a spectator, based on the sheer generosity of your imagination), that following an athletic event and feeling united with athletes and the crowd can yield some of the more addictively uplifting moments of our lives, do you think there is anything specific about watching sports that goes beyond these moments? Is there anything that remains, anything you can carry home or cash out once the intensity of an athletic event ebbs away? Throughout this book, I have insisted that I find it praiseworthy enough if those athletic moments are just as good as only they can be, and that they do not need any justification in words or in the currency of practical gains. But it is one thing to be convinced of a position you argue, and another thing to naively expect others to agree. So in a mildly preemptive closing move, I want to address the anticipated objection—that watching sports is pure and pointless hedonism—and react to it with the serenity of those who are certain of a value they may never be able to explain fully to anyone else.

To answer this question, let us back up a minute and ask the same thing about the yield, for everyday life, of actually *playing* sports. When we ask why it is good to practice sports, and if we put aside for the moment preventive health as an answer, then what we are likely to hear, at least within the world of Anglo-American college sports, is that being an athlete "builds character."

But however plausible the connection may seem to be between exposing oneself to the rigors of athletic practice and, say, developing good work habits, the investment and sacrifices required are just too huge and the results too unspecific to make practicing sports with the goal of building one's character a good trade-off. And besides, even if it worked for athletes, it does not work for spectators, whose physical sacrifices are minimal, if one can call them sacrifices at all.

So we are back to asking, once again, whether there is anything beyond sheer pleasure that we spectators inadvertently and unknowingly gain by watching sports. One answer that I want to pursue in these closing remarks, is this: from a long career of watching sports, what I have "gained" is a strong, though not well identified, feeling of gratitude toward the athletes who have given me so many special moments of intensity. My gratitude could be described as "intransitive" because I do not exactly know what it is, on the athletes' side, that I should and could be personally thankful for. Without a doubt, my favorite athletes did not perform for me specifically or for any other spectators whom they did not know. They followed their own urge to compete and to strive for excellence, and perhaps even their own practical reasons. So how do I explain this feeling of gratitude toward athletes? For what am I grateful?

Here is my heartfelt and yet tentative answer. Under present-day conditions, in a culture that has a sharper awareness than any culture before about the limits of human performance, and that also has more efficient ways of using this knowledge to reach those limits, watching sports is a way of waiting for that which may occasionally happen but is never guaranteed to happen, because it lies beyond the precalculated limits of human performance. To let happen and to see happen, occasionally, what we have no right to expect—this may indeed be the kind of experience toward which we fans are open when we watch sports.

Ancient Greek culture had a (then highly convincing) way to explain how that which was not supposed to occur sometimes did. For the Greeks, surprising feats happened in the presence of gods, through divine intervention, and this is why Greek athletes who achieved the unexpected and the overwhelmingly great sometimes appeared to be transfigured into demigods. But for those who do

not believe in the possibility of such divine inter-
cession, to celebrate athletic events as the happening of that which exceeds our expectations can
turn into a somehow paradoxical celebration of the
limits of human performance and perhaps even
into a celebration of the randomness that occasionally beats these limits. It is a paradoxical celebration because, different from other moments of
its kind, celebrating the overcoming of a limit does
not imply that this limit will cease to exist in the
future. On the contrary, celebrating the exception
to a limitation ends up being its affirmation. And
yet we appreciate the randomness that makes such
exceptions possible. At the Olympics or in a world
championship, few joys are greater than witnessing
the "impossible" upset victory of an underdog athlete or a wild card team that was never supposed to
win, and indeed may never perform at the same
level again.

This idea—never performing at the same level
again—brings up a second explanation for my
feeling of gratitude toward athletes. Being able to
make the impossible happen can have devastating
consequences (the word is not too strong) for athletes after their retirement. Why do top athletes

have such a difficult time quitting their sport? Why did Michael Jordan, perhaps the greatest basketball player of all time, end his career and then return to uniform not just once but twice, ignoring the inevitable negative effect this would have on his legend and even his wealth? Why did Mario Lemieux, one of the greatest hockey players ever, not retire from the Pittsburgh Penguins earlier, before disappointed fans were forced to compare the all-too-present aging Lemieux with their memories of his former glory? One answer is that modern society has no good solution or convincing strategy for the postcareer existence of great athletes. Most world-class athletes turn into waste once their careers are over. By using the word waste, what I refer to is not only the deplorably frequent but always isolated cases of irreversible physical damage so movingly portrayed in Clint Eastwood's *Million Dollar Baby*. I am speaking of waste above all in a psychological or cultural sense.

A broad range of self-declared solutions for retired athletes has emerged, but none of them takes care of the key problem at hand, which is how to make a smooth transition from being a demigod to being a normal person. Jordan's and Lemieux's answer—trying to avoid the impossible transition by indefinitely postponing it—is nothing less than a way of dying alive. Babe Ruth followed the same road. After the New York Yankees, whose fame he had almost single-handedly created, made it unmercifully clear by 1935 that they had no use for him anymore, he joined the Boston Braves, but his performance became a less than sorry shadow of his once glorious self. Ruth spent the last years of his life waiting, day after day, for an offer from a baseball franchise to become its manager, but the call never came. Even those former athletes who do become coaches—quite often player-coaches like Jordan and Lemieux—hardly ever end up being happy in their new situation. Remaining a bit player in a world they once dominated makes it all the more painfully obvious how normal they have become, and how impossible it is for them to transmit the unique talent they no longer have to the lesser athletes they must now mentor.

The cleanest and most demanding solution, the one chosen by Joe DiMaggio, comes at the opposite price, the price of self-erasure. DiMaggio dropped completely out of sight after the end of his professional career. He became invisible, spending his life withdrawn from the world, hidden behind walls of agents who administered whatever assets were left from his public life. Sandy Koufax continues to follow this path today.

Occasionally a world-class athlete becomes highly respected in some other field of endeavor. Roger Bannister, the first athlete to run the mile in less than four minutes, became an outstanding neurologist. And Diana Nyad, who in the 1970s was the greatest long-distance swimmer in the world, embarked upon a brilliant career in television, radio, and print commentary. Some former athletes not only manage to preserve the fortune they accumulated during their active years but even to increase it, and to climb several steps up the social hierarchy in the process. George Foreman, after retiring as the world heavyweight boxing champion, became a minister and then turned his hand to making millions of dollars with his George Foreman Grill.

Ted Williams of the Boston Red Sox, perhaps the all-time greatest hitter in baseball, with his 1941 season average of .406, quit twice to volunteer for World War II and the Korean War, where he distinguished himself as a pilot. But the ups and downs in the postcareer life of this American war hero—his divorces and family feuds, his failures as a baseball manager, and his strange diseases—remained painfully public right up through the bizarre circumstances surrounding his death and cryogenic preservation in 2002.

Franz Beckenbauer, without any doubt the greatest and most famous player in the history of German soccer, reached an even higher level of respect by successfully coaching the national soccer team to one vice championship and one championship of the world. He was instrumental in bringing the 2006 soccer World Cup to Germany, and few if any German politicians would not proudly claim that they enjoy his friendship. Yet Beckenbauer, once a player of proverbially un-German elegance, is now just an average German multimillionaire who attends the annual opera festival at Bayreuth (one of the most exclusive cultural events in his country) as eagerly and proudly as any other cultivated *bourgeois.* Comparing these accomplishments to the unforgettable matches he once played, I somehow cannot help, "against better knowledge," finding his postretirement achievements offputting. The postcareer plans that fail most miserably, I indeed think, are the very ones that journalists and proud fans often hail as the "good solutions."

But is the more philistine life of so many retired soccer stars in Europe a better solution? During the glorious soccer decades of the mid-twentieth century, former top players would be trusted with tobacco shops or gas stations, and in some more eminent cases with a roadside restaurant or a movie theater. Today, their successors become sales reps and later on maybe regional directors for brands like Adidas, Puma, or Nike. Occasionally they lend their names to a column in the tabloid press or become TV specialists for their former sport, always either too silent or too helplessly loquacious. Many fans like to see their stars in such reincarnations because they find it comforting to realize that former demigods have become "people like you and me." For my part, I would rather have kept my memories of the incomparably threatening forward Ferenc Puskas at a discreet distance from his reborn image as an overweight sweaty producer of Hungarian sausages in Madrid.

Some would say that such respectable middle-class choices are quite encouraging, especially if we see them in contrast with the countless stars whose lives, in different degrees of scandal, simply went to shambles or ended much too soon. Many of these athletes wind up in dramatically deteriorated health, under the lingering suspicion that physical decline was the price they paid for those years of bodily stress. When Babe Ruth made his last appearance in Yankee Stadium during the 1948 season, his voice failing from throat cancer, everyone blamed it on baseball players' notorious addiction to chewing tobacco.

If Jesse Owens's death from lung cancer in 1980 was just an average smoker's fate, the forty-four years that remained to him after his triumphs in the 1936 Olympics were marked by a long series of failures. These failures were all the more frustrating because, at most stages of his life, some well-intentioned public gestures of support were made to help him out. Hoping to cash in on his Olympic success with amounts of money that look pathetic today, Owens lost his amateur status and had to file bankruptcy by 1939. Desperate to make a living, he indiscriminately accepted all kinds of offers that promised financial yield. He ran against race horses, he supported the Republican party in

election campaigns, and whenever he was asked
(and paid) he offered benevolent backing to political causes of the African-American population. After being pursued and finally cleared by the FBI on
charges of being a Communist in the early 1950s,
Owens became an official envoy of the American
president to the 1956 Olympics at Melbourne. He
started several new business ventures and ended
up, once again, in financial ruin by the early 1960s.
All of this did not prevent official America from
showering Jesse Owens with distinction. He received an honorary doctorate from Ohio State
University, his alma mater, in 1972; the Medal of
Freedom was bestowed by President Gerald Ford
in 1976; and President Jimmy Carter named him
a Living Legend of the United States in 1979.
Owens's "legendary" accomplishments were too
precious a promotional tool for politicians to ig-
nore, but when he was not in the spotlight, his
post-Olympic life was almost always in some kind
of trouble.

The word "tragic" is not too strong to describe
the fate of Muhammad Ali, who was most likely
right when he called himself the greatest boxer of
all times. The neurological disorder from which he

suffers today is most likely a direct consequence of
his career as a boxer. Some specialists even claim
that his injury can be traced specifically to the
pounding Ali took in his three epic fights against
Joe Frazier in the 1970s. All the edifying literature
published about Ali since his retirement from the
ring will not convince those who saw him challenge U.S. authority during his younger years that
he is now leading a happy, conflict-free life. In order to secure a trouble-free existence for his family
and himself, Ali seems constantly obliged to make
concessions. At the opening ceremony of the otherwise unglamorous 1996 games at Atlanta, when
Ali, with his painfully slow movements and his ex-
pressionless face, lit the Olympic fire, two con-
flicting interpretations came to my mind. The op-
timistic interpretation was that no other person in
the world could have managed, as Ali did, to draw
the attention of billions of fans to the problems of
people with disabilities, and to teach those fans
that even small movements performed by a handi-
capped body can be an amazing athletic achievement. But what nobody dared to say explicitly was
that Ali probably had no real choice. The man
whose physical prowess had enchanted several gen-

erations of spectators was now paying a price for his greatness, not only by living in a body made dysfunctional by his sport, but also by agreeing—by most probably feeling that he had to agree, for the sake of his family's security—to showcase that failing body for the entire world, as he had once showcased his younger self.

The racism that the young Ali was so determined to fight—and did fight, with great personal risk and admirable success—was the downfall of other athletes. Jim Thorpe, the son of an Irish father and a Native American mother, won the pentathlon and the decathlon at the Stockholm Olympic games in 1912, and the anecdote is often told that the Swedish king congratulated him for being "the greatest athlete on earth." Less than a year later, the American Olympic committee denounced Thorpe for doing what so many white Olympians had done without penalty: accepting a small amount of money for playing baseball. He was forced to give back his Olympic medals, and he spent the rest of his life as an alcoholic, drifting between the reservation and an urban underworld of cheap entertainment. Thorpe's biography ended on a grotesque note: in 1953 his widow sold his corpse to a village in Pennsylvania (where he had never lived) so that his remains could buried there and the town would rename itself after the great athlete.

More typical than histories of painful victimage are the lives of former world-class athletes who gave in to their own self-destructive impulses. We live in the presence of hundreds of them today, and occasionally even read about their fate. Mike Tyson, former heavyweight champion of the world, is a particularly famous case. Now middle-aged and poorly managed, the Mike Tyson whose threatening outbursts were so enjoyable to watch at a TV distance in the 1980s will probably never be able to pay off the millions of dollars in debt he owes because nobody is particularly interested anymore in seeing him lose yet another fight. Likewise, Darryl Strawberry, one of the most talented baseball players of the generation now beginning to enter retirement, may never liberate himself from the downward spiral of probation deadlines, drug dependency, cancer treatments, and staggering debt in which he seems trapped.

Diego Maradona, the most explosive soccer forward to play during my lifetime, fought his way back from cocaine addiction and is currently heading a TV show in Argentina, but his rocky transition to a less-than-heroic existence nearly killed him. Gerd Müller, who retired in 1982 after a career in which he scored more improbable goals for West Germany than any other player, will probably never live independently again. A serious alcohol problem left his life in ruins, and he might not have survived without the mercy of his former teammates, who are now making millions by running Bayern Munich, the team that Müller kicked into European eminence.

The fate of Werner Kohlmeyer was similar. This left defender, who stopped a shot on the goal line in the last minute of the final that Germany won for the country's first soccer World Cup in 1954, was often the target of his teammates' practical jokes. Captain Fritz Walter narrates in his autobiography how, on the flight back from Germany's first international match ever in the Soviet Union, he and the other players managed to squeeze into Kohlmeyer's suitcase all the guinea pigs that the team had received as presents from their Communist hosts. Sadly, the game at Moscow would be one of Kohlmeyer's last on the national team. A few months later, his alcohol problems overwhelmed him; but unlike Müller, he refused the charitable offers of help from his former teammates and coaches. Fifty years old and on the payroll of a local newspaper as a parking lot attendant, Kohlmeyer died of heart failure in 1974, shortly before Germany won the soccer World Cup for a second time.

Kohlmeyer's life strikes me as a modest German parallel to the miserable life of Manuel Francisco dos Santos who, as Mané Garrincha, played on the teams that won Brazil's first two World Cups in 1958 and 1962 and was simply the best right winger of all times. He was born in a slum called Pau Grande on the periphery of Rio de Janeiro. Like Wilma Rudolph, he miraculously overcame walking and growing problems in his childhood that had left his legs bowed. Garrincha, his stadium name, referred to this very visible defect and to his sparrow-like constitution—but it also carried a connotation of being easygoing and naïve. Nothing made Garrincha prouder than showing off his VW Beetle in Pau Grande, which indicates how scandalously underpaid he was, even by late-1950s standards in Brazil.

Garrincha's soccer repertoire consisted of just one fast and not very complex trick. He let his body drift to one side and then suddenly passed with the ball on the other side, thus fooling all the great defenders of his era. They knew Garrincha's trick, as did the spectators in every soccer country of the world, but he was impossible to stop. Garrincha became so obsessed with fooling his opponents over and over again that he often forgot to pass or to shoot at the right moment. Having become an alcoholic by the time he was thirty years old, Garrincha played for an endless string of teams all over South America, sometimes for just one game before he was traded away for being intoxicated. Like Kohlmeyer, who might well have been trusted with covering Garrincha had Brazil ever played Germany during those years, he died miserably at the age of fifty from alcohol-induced heart failure.

The star on the Uruguay soccer team that won the Olympic tournaments of 1924 in Paris and 1928 at Amsterdam and went on to triumph in the first soccer World Cup in Montevideo in 1930 was José Leandro Andrade. Go to any website listing the top twenty greatest soccer players of all time and you will find the name of José Leandro Andrade among them. Although this is never explicitly mentioned (because soccer likes to present itself as if exempt from history), Andrade, more than any other player during the first third of the twentieth century, put soccer on the map of international sports. The very few photographs of him—mostly in collective portraits of the dominating Uruguayan team—show him as the only black player, standing a bit taller than most of his teammates (we know that he measured more than six feet, which was very exceptional by soccer standards, and indeed by any standards, of his time). He always wore knee protectors on both legs, his body was perfectly shaped, and unlike most other players he never showed a smile. Andrade looked very serious and confident in those photographs.

Most of the surviving documents about his soccer career refer to the Olympic games of 1924 at Paris where, thanks to the Uruguayan players who beat Switzerland 3:0 in the final, soccer became a central attraction, probably for the first time ever, at an important international sports event. Nobody fascinated the spectators in the Stade Colombes more than José Leandro Andrade, as the

Montevideo daily *El Día* proudly reported in an article of June 11: "Leandro is the 'hero,' the bard, the 'man of unbelievable legs,' the 'fantastic one.' Do you believe, dear reader that those who speak about him in these words are exaggerating? If you do, you are simply wrong. Andrade deservedly inspires all these expressions. It is impossible to speak or to write about him without such hyperbolic words dropping from your pen."

After the arrival of his team in Europe a few weeks before the opening of the Olympics, and during a tour of several matches played against Spanish major league clubs, everybody on his team seemed to be either excited or jealous about the countless love letters and amorous advances that Andrade received. Those were the years when not only intellectuals in Europe discovered African beauty and grace. Andrade was also a good enough dancer of the popular Argentinian and Uruguayan tangos to make credible the rumor that he had received offers to appear on the stages of Parisian cabarets.

And what did Andrade's soccer look like? The sobering answer is that we do not know—and, most probably, we will never know. There is some footage of the 1924 Olympics final, but it does not provide a distinctive impression of his athletic style. All the written descriptions of Andrade's game are too enthusiastic and generic to have much value for our imagination. Our picture of Andrade the athlete resembles our picture of the origin of the universe: we can still detect waves from that long-ago cosmic explosion, but as we look out in space and back in time, the event itself is forever just beyond our visible horizon. Similarly, we have traces of a sensational athletic energy emanating from Andrade's performance, but not what we would call a visual memory. All that is left from his game are those fading waves of hyperbolic admiration and intense desire, together with a few dry facts. We know that Andrade played half back, a position similar to the one that Zidane and Ronaldinho (who bears a certain physical resemblance to Andrade) play. Like good midfielders today, Andrade covered certain defensive functions at the same time. As is typical for this position, he scored only occasionally, but all eyewitnesses were enchanted with the effortless elegance in his movements. Andrade was famous for never celebrating goals on the field and for hardly ever participating in team practice. Often he did not even show up at gametime, which may explain why he participated in only about half of the games that his national team played between 1923 and 1930.

Almost everything else that is known about Andrade's life has become part of his mythology. He was born at Salto, a small town in northern Uruguay, close to the Brazilian border, on October 1, 1901. His mother was Argentinean. José Ignacio Andrade, whose name appears as a witness on the birth certificate and who was most likely his father, was ninety-eight years old when Leandro was born; he had probably come to Brazil in his youth as a slave from West Africa, and he later escaped from a farm in southern Brazil. The father made a living as an expert in magic rituals of African origin, especially love charms.

When exactly his son moved from Salto to Montevideo and from what date he began to play soccer for money, more or less unofficially, is unclear. Rumor has it that he was also occasionally working as a gigolo in the harbor district of the city. By 1923, however, he was on the Uruguayan team that won a South American championship. Having stayed at Paris for several months after the great Olympic triumph of 1924, Andrade joined Nacional Montevideo in 1925, which is still today (with Peñarol) one of the two outstanding Uruguyan soccer franchises, for another tour in Europe. It was during that tour, at Brussels in May 1925, that he was diagnosed with syphilis. Andrade returned to Montevideo ahead of his new teammates, and immediately upon his arrival at Montevideo harbor on July 22, among rumors about his deteriorating health, he gave one of the few interviews of his life to a reporter, who described him this way:

> At first glance, José Leandro Andrade with whom we had the opportunity to conduct a brief conversation does not look affected by a serious disease. He seems to have lost some weight compared to his departure from Montevideo but he does definitely not look suffering. Once we talked to him, the impression changed. Andrade is parsimonious with his words and those who have known him for some time believe to see an air of depression in his face. We ask about his health and Andrade answers: "I returned because I feel

somewhat ill, and I will follow a treatment here in order to fully recover as soon as possible. Here in Montevideo, I have the certainty that things will go smoothly. I trust our local doctors more than the doctors abroad."

Things would never again go smoothly for Andrade. Feeling constantly tired, he just barely made the Uruguyan team that won its second gold medal in 1928 in Holland. That he still ended up being on the first world championship team in 1930 was perhaps due more to the journalists' and spectators' expectations than to the quality of his game. All we know for a fact is that the ever-growing soccer crowds of those years still wanted to see the black world star Andrade. After the Montevideo World Cup, however, his game and his health disintegrated permanently. Although José Leandro Andrade lived for almost three more decades, he was incapable of ever holding a job, and he seems to have gone through all the merciless stages of syphilitic decay. Three days after his fifty-seventh birthday, on October 4, 1958, he died. His corpse was laid out at the home of his sister Nicasia, the mother of Víctor Rodríguez Andrade, who played on the team that, against all odds, won Uruguay's second World Cup against Brazil at Rio de Janeiro's Maracana Stadium in 1950.

So far, this concluding section has had the structure of a litany. In a sustained reiteration, it has evoked names from the past whose parallel fates have all been disappointing, many of them bordering on tragedy. But while these accumulated mini-biographies converge in showing how, so often, the lives of top athletes become waste, I hope they have triggered an impulse of gratitude in you, at least those among you who enjoy watching sports as much as I do and may therefore have seen some of those athletes when they were in their prime. As I said at the beginning, I find this gratitude, at least my own gratitude toward the athletes I have mentioned here, strangely intransitive. Intransitive in some, historically remote cases, like the one of José Leandro Andrade, because we do not know—and will never know—what kind of performance awakened such strong waves of almost erotic desire. Intransitive also even in the case of Mané Garrincha, my all-time favorite soccer player whose moves and tricks I pride myself on remembering with almost documentary precision. Yes, I wish Garrincha had had a better life and a less miserable death—but even if he were still around, as a well-preserved seventy-something Brazilian national icon, what is the likelihood that I could shake his hand in gratitude and tell him, which is true, that few things in my life have given me such pleasure as his stunningly beautiful plays? And if I could, what would be the point?

For the longest time, I have not been able to find an answer to this question, which in the end converges with the question why we should praise athletic beauty at all. Then, for reasons completely unrelated to my interest in sports, I reread an interview given by a former colleague whom I greatly admired as an intellectual, a novelist, and a poet. This was the eminent medievalist Paul Zumthor, whose presence and wisdom I have often missed since his death in 1995. Asked about his personal motivation for an unheard-of explosion of intellectual productivity during his retirement years, Zumthor gave the following answer:

> I am trying to convince myself that it is not
> my responsibility and not even my problem
> if, one day, my health, some random circum-

stances, or my fate will make it impossible for me to continue working—and will ultimately be my death. What I do accept as my responsibility is quite different indeed: it lies in imagining projects for my work so that, through them, I can keep myself in life; and if possible at all, this responsibility also lies in trying to finish these projects and thus to show life that I love it.

Paul Zumthor made me understand that remembering Jesse Owens, Wilma Rudolph, and Mané Garrincha, praising the past grace of Muhammad Ali, trying to make present again Akebono's and Diego Maradona's performance, has been a way of expressing gratitude for the life that I have and that I am enjoying. Praising athletic beauty responds to this impulse of gratitude—but it has to remain intransitive, without individual addressees. As my words will never reach the ear of my former heroes and as I have no gods to pray to, what I write may indeed turn into "gratitude toward life." It could turn into something as private—and some would say as pointless—as "showing life that I love it."

For making such effusive statements I have been both welcomed and criticized, in recent years, as an "inadvertent religious thinker" and as promoting "a strange kind of vitalism." Well, why not— but then again, why? While I do not actively avoid it, I certainly find myself unable to engage in anything that can be called a religion. At the same time, it is true that I have long been melancholic and sometimes even upset about the very cerebral tone of speaking and writing among academics (although I no doubt am a very typical incarnation of this life form). Could it be the case that I watch athletes—and love to admire them—in the sense of that most famous concept of love from Plato's *Symposium*? Are athletes, for me, in their grace and elegance, with their violence and their unsuitedness for normal life, that "other half" of myself that I have not managed to claim and become?

This was the fantasy with which I intended to finish my book, when my friend the philosopher Martin Seel wrote to me that he finds it "a funny idea" that we fall in love because we want to complete ourselves, and he reminded me how strange it would be to end a book in praise of athletic beauty by conjuring up Plato as the ultimate icon of philosophical idealism. Martin then gave me the words that I should have found myself to conclude: "By watching sports, we can enjoy, in our imagination, certain lives that we have neither the talent nor the time to live." And to be grateful for such possibilities, as Miguel Tamen wrote to me on the same day only a few minutes later than Seel, "sometimes shows that there is something all right with us, that our earthly transit is not marked by resentment but by enthusiasm and admiration, by a sense that what happens is more important than the sense that it has happened to ourselves." I am content to end my hymn in praise of athletic beauty on these borrowed notes, and grateful, in a very transitive way, to my friends for so generously lending their words when my own started to fail.

ACKNOWLEDGMENTS

THIS BOOK SPEAKS, on its final pages, about the gratitude I feel toward so many former and present athletes—a gratitude for "keeping me in life" that I will most likely never manage to bring to the attention of those I watch and admire with such passion. Fortunately, gratitude is not always of necessity intransitive. I would like to take this opportunity to express a more transitive feeling of appreciation to friends and colleagues who, for many years, have patiently, benevolently supported my work on sports and helped me share my enthusiasm, in ways that have been as vitalizing as an afternoon in the stadium.

I want to begin by thanking those scholars from whose essays and books I have learned so much, without ever mentioning them by name. For reasons that I hope are self-evident, *In Praise of Athletic Beauty* became footnote-free, but I could never have been written it without the insights of Allen Guttmann, who is simply the master of all sports historians; Glenn Most, who, without being a fan, wrote more inspiringly about ancient Greek athletes than less competent enthusiasts ever could; and Gunter Gebauer, with whom I agree on hardly anything about sports but whose thoughts I admire and whose trenchant arguments I have often had reason to fear. And I would like to remember the late Josef Göhler, whose high-bar routines made my teenage classmates and me feel that even a scholar can love the performance of beautiful bodies.

Among the many friends who engaged in intense discussions with me while I was writing, two have generously shared more ideas than I could ever begin to acknowledge here: the uncannily sharp Martin Seel and the uncannily intuitive Miguel Tamen. I want to include in this *Légion d'honneur* of intellectual sponsorship my through-the-carrel-wall neighbor Bliss Carnochan, for making me rewrite more than one entire chapter (which at first I didn't like doing one bit); Felicitas Noeske, for being authoritative but never authoritarian; Nico Pethes, for not al-

lowing me to become untheoretical; Lucia Prauscello,
for caring about how much sleep I got (at Green Library and at home); Henning Ritter, for referring me
to more good books than my slow-reading self could
ever digest; and Michel Zink, for pointing out that
the number of players on a soccer team is not all that
obvious.

Some other friends intervened with the intellectual
equivalent of a "clean hit": I thank Karl Heinz Bohrer
for keeping me from running away with easy opinions about aesthetics; Horst Bredekamp for saving
me from complacency (by telling an august German
assembly that Michelangelo would have admired
Jesse Owens); Monika Fick for caring about her
friends' passions; Nina Buhre for displaying a competence whose timeliness exceeds the visual; Ruben
Gallo for showing me so many stadiums, when they
really mattered; Chris, for working on my style;
Marco, for a "set up" (as a concept and almost a
thing); Yasushi Ishii for commentaries that kept me
going (although I never really understood them); to
Joachim Küpper and Andreas Kablitz for a delightful
conversation (not about sports) at just the right moment; Ulla Link-Heer for making it rain when I was
talking; Aldo Mazzucchelli for nothing less than

Andrade's life and beautiful Spanish words; Thomas Pavel for a circus (being a circus); Ludwig Pfeiffer for agreeing to disagree, mainly in spirit (because in an athletic competition I couldn't keep up with him anyway); Irina Prokharova for laughing at my very academic jokes; to Mads Rosendahl for helping me see Stanford basketball from the perspective of Copenhagen; Violeta Sánchez for some fighting bulls; Sara, for being a *Sternchen;* Bernhard Siegert for Weimarer Kulturtechnik; Ellen Todd for referring me to Federer's "gestures"; Michael Walter for continuing to be no-nonsense; David Wellbery, for mercilessly polite sharpness; and Wolfgang Welsch for sharing the passion with superior composure.

Some people help a writer write by simply letting him believe they would like to read his words, even when the writer knows, deep-down, that they have much better things to do. Champions in this complex and much-underestimated art are Chi Elliott, who found my style minimalist; Petra Hardt, who managed to make me remember (and then let me forget again) that books also are things to be sold; Brigitte Landes, who should remain what she already is, a beacon of inspirational magic; and Arnold Rampersad, whose dignity I admire even more than his biographies. I also want to thank Bernd Stiegler for his intensely light expectations; Margaret Tompkins, for, among many things, her belief that Sam can play for Stanford or USC; and Rainer Weiss, who, for all the good reasons on earth, relied on Egon Loy rather than the Christmas market.

Susan Wallace Boehmer, cutting right through professorial narcissism with the elegance of a surgeon and the charm of an intellectual aristocrat, made me believe that my manuscript was worth the investment of yet another summer, as she helped me to like some of its less academic "moments." But she would not have had the opportunity to do so had Lindsay Waters not smelled sloppiness in the first place (no other human being can smell sloppiness better!). I also want to acknowledge my students and colleagues from the School of Critical Theory at Cornell University, who in the summer of 2005 put up with the rewriting of a book whose content they had no chance to grasp. With Robbie Harrison (who taught me how much it matters to know about dying) I had hardly ever spoken about this book before it was done; but to know that he was betting on it made up for a religious obligation.

Like its sponsoring institution, the (no-longer-existing) building of Stanford-at-Kyoto was an ideal place to be lost-in-writing. During my stay there, Eiko Fujioka introduced me to the Hanshin Tigers; Erin Gardener managed to fool me every morning; Kenny Gundle had a smoke on the patio, despite his ecological commitments; Lisa Honda chose the very best sake; Shawn Standefer knew when I really needed to talk; and Anjou Chen was just an all-round class act, even though she left for Harvard.

But once again, there was no better place in the world (at least for me) to write than Stanford University because no other place can beat ancient Greece (and I mean it) in making athletics and academics one. This miracle happens every day throughout the year, thanks to people like Seyi Aboleji, whose passes are as smooth as his mind is razor-sharp; Matt Doyle, who embodies what is best about this university; Josh Landy, who doesn't allow me ever to forget soccer; Ted Leland, who by being a genius and looking like a football coach kept things together; Trina Marmarelli, who makes the rhythms of ballgames converge with those of poetry; Pablo Morales, who gave mute humanists the tongues of athletes; Rick Schavone, who never ceases to try something new; Matthew Tiews, who came back; Bill Walsh, who talked about European and American fans on flights to Annapolis; coach Walt Harris, who knows (like I do) how much it is a guys' thing to love scents; and Coach Tyrone Willingham, whose greatness stayed and will forever be present with us.

Ricky, Sara, and Laura are more beautiful and more exciting to me than the greatest plays that I have ever seen emerge—and unlike plays they never vanish.